EMOTIONAL RAGS to SPIRITUAL RICHES

EMOTIONAL RAGS to SPIRITUAL RICHES

A Personal Story of the Rags of Addiction and the Spiritual Gifts of Recovery

DAVID GREGORY

EMOTIONAL RAGS TO SPIRITUAL RICHES
A PERSONAL STORY OF THE RAGS OF ADDICTION
AND THE SPIRITUAL GIFTS OF RECOVERY

iUniverse books may be ordered through booksellers or by contacting:

iUniverse
1663 Liberty Drive
Bloomington, IN 47403
www.iuniverse.com
844-349-9409

ISBN: 978-1-5320-0109-3 (sc)
ISBN: 978-1-5320-0110-9 (hc)
ISBN: 978-1-5320-0111-6 (e)

Library of Congress Control Number: 2016910398

Print information available on the last page.

iUniverse rev. date: 11/02/2023

This book is dedicated to the millions of people world wide that are gifted with addiction as a wake up call to change their lives just by being willing.

I thank Judy Richards and Judy Furman for their incredible gift of editing and to all the souls that guided me along the way of my own re-birthing.

I now know that I have always been lovingly cared for by the Universe and that the God of my understanding has always had my back even at a time that I was unaware.

WHAT WE THINK IS WHAT WE GET

Doesn't everyone love and relate to a great "Rags to Riches" story? How about a journey that was started in the dysfunction of a family already laced with addiction and mental illness? A story that was true and the only medication to make it through the scars left behind was alcohol. But with hiding the one of two diseases, the first being one that beat down an already troubled soul, took away all self-esteem, was punished with verbal abuse and lack of love, and then the second disease kicked in. It was a family disease that had been documented over the last generation. This disease took the life of a father by suicide. This disease left a family in constant fear and shambles. It was a disease that ran rampant throughout both sides of the family. It affected cousins and aunts and uncles and was creating a milder effect in the story you are going to read, but it definitely took its toll and the illnesses and early deaths were proof of the consequences of the deadly diseases of addiction to alcohol and prescription drugs.

Since the movie industry began, stories such as this one always seem to get top billing in movie theaters. They are typically best sellers at the local bookstore. Of course they are! They are sensational and usually pretty close to home. We all like to think that we can pull ourselves out of a sinkhole of addiction, and end up on a mountaintop. And… we can, but it takes and takes, and it is not easy to leave the Rags of addiction to find the Riches in our nirvana.

Living in the throes of addiction and the Emotional Rags that go with it can cause us to experience a great deal of fear, but many times we don't recognize the fear enough to pull ourselves out of it. That is unless we hit such a low bottom that there is nowhere else to go except to die. If we choose not to die, we have a fighting chance to dig out.

How do we magically transform our Emotional Rags into Spiritual Riches? And what it this thing we are talking about called Emotional Rags?

Emotional Rags are all the many things in life that we go through on a day to day basis even without the cravings for drink. They are the Rags of what we think are the fears of loss, the fears of being defeated, lied to, abandoned

1

and so on. When we are in addiction the fears and abandonment issues are ten times greater. Addiction is a huge emotional rag that tries to find a way out with a liquid that leaves us numb and totally unaccountable for actions that we place on others who are usually our care-takers. Who needs to change a baby's diaper after they are potty trained? Who needs to monitor an alcoholic who is irresponsible, unfaithful, and not able to keep a life together for themselves or the family and friends they are constantly affecting.

We all have Rags in our lives but the alcoholic does not want to know about the Rags, will not address the Rags, and buries his head in the sand with lies and delusional thinking. It is never their fault for anything and whether they are a happy or a mean drunk, this is the same message they carry. They are not responsible but their life and their jobs, and their health and… and… and… are what are making them drink. There is no fixing the Rags of addiction until the addicted one is ready to go the road to recovery.

Save your breath, you have no power over the alcoholic. The more you pull them out of their problems, the longer it takes them to hit a bottom so they can feel their needed fall. A fall that hurts so much, they are finally ready to surrender and listen. They are ready to do whatever it takes to never ever pick up a drink or a drug again.

Enabling an alcoholic can ruin the lives of those trying so desperately to save them. The drink or drug will always win over the one trying to help. And when there is no one around, they can find their drug of choice quickly and efficiently and will be drunk or drugged quickly without remorse. That is, until the hangover kicks in and they need more. Until they have had enough, they will not stop and do not want to stop no matter what they may tell you. This is a cunning and powerful disease of the body, mind and spirit.

There are two people that we find we are talking to. One is the drunk. The other is the drunk that will tell us anything to get that drink or drug. They will also be very convincing that they do not have a problem but you do, if they cannot get what they want.

Until they surrender there is no helping them. However, once a true surrender out of desperation happens, is when they are ready to address the disease and then they can finally be supported and loved. But this is a different kind of love. This is a love of support. This is a love of standing next to them and encouraging them to change one thing. Everything. This is the time when they will finally see you and know you as being a support person in their court. But not until they are ready.

The Rags are to teach us a better way of thinking, feeling and doing so that we can experience our Riches. The Riches are the times when we are finally content even for a moment. The Riches are the times we breathe easier and know that we are safe, guided, and loved with extravagance and that we always have been and always will be.

When experiencing the Rags, any kind of Emotional Rag, we as humans seem to create stories based on our past and future fears...along with feelings of deficiencies. As a result, we become hesitant to move forward in our lives. We become frustrated, and many times feel hopeless and "wanting." Wanting what? We don't know.

A good success story about "Rags to Riches" is often glorified at the movies, but when we sit at home and are alone pondering dilemmas, we face that clear-cut reality of not knowing how to get out of the Rags of our daily lives. We want the success of those Riches but are we really willing to take the leap and "let" it happen?

The leap, when finally done, is an obvious life change. The Riches we had been seeking are like a lion ready to jump out of a cage to return to freedom. With time and changes in thinking, money, relationships, and professions that we have secretly stuffed in our desire bag, start showing signs of coming true. It does take diligence and a steady walk without looking back and omitting the temptation to look forward but we will see and feel a deep change in purpose. These dilemmas that we felt in the Rags of our life, we come to realize were ego driven from an ego that chattered away not at our opportunities but focused on all of our adversities along the way, keeping us fearful to admit need for change and then move forward to do the change. With the unhealthy ego hard at work, we tend to hear a very commanding voice telling us that we are not worthy and that it cannot be done. But is this also our own way of staying lazy with a recovery mode? Are we talking ourselves out of our own good so that we can stay mired in our own addictive ways of thinking? Why would we let anything, including ourselves, or our lives as they are, not change?

The answer found for most of us is that we have started and stopped so many times in an effort to change our way of living that we are afraid. We are afraid that we cannot do this change of thinking. And for the first time in a long time, we are absolutely right. We cannot do this by ourselves. It will take surrender to something much bigger than ourself. And that surrender is what will give us consistent sobriety, free from drama and relapsing, because when we finally turn it over…everything over, we are free to heal.

We lose the obsession that we truly will not have what we want and what we need. *Why?* Would we believe that we are not worthy to receive the gift of Spiritual Riches? If we look closely, we will see that our head, not our heart, is controlling our life. The heart is the answer to everything when we connect to our Senior Partner, the God of our understanding. For far too long many of us have accepted life for what we THINK it is, not what it could be. And with this kind of thinking, we want to medicate with a mind altering drug to silence the chattering doom and gloom that our unhealthy chattering ego wants to fill us up with. Who would not look for relief? None of us want to live with this pain and chatter. So we find out how to close ourselves down and how to stop thinking so that we can have some peace. Checking out of life for a while works but then comes the day when it does not. And when we have checked out for a period of time, we have only added more pain in the form of acting out without hesitation, destroying relationships, losing credibility in the work place. Most of all, when we are sober we have to see who we really are. That is enough to take another drug or a drink. We cross the line and can no longer stay sober for any period of time.

4

Every one of us gets the chance to change and grow and become the truth of who we are. Alcohol is a big wakeup call along with drugs. But alcoholics many times fail to realize this is a time when many will turn to medicating with drugs, alcohol, food, and sex in an addictive way to forget what they have chattering in their heads. But something happens in the Emotional Rags of addiction that changes our lives. We continue to get our wake up calls. Sometimes they are subtle and as we ignore the messages they seem to get a little harder to miss until they are not hard to miss at all. This is the bottom that some of us have to hit to get our attention.

When the addiction we are in is no longer working, we have only two ways to go. We can choose to go nowhere resulting in taking a life or taking our own. The other option is to change the way we think. But after years of thinking a certain way, it will take effort, commitment and faith to overcome this insidious disease. It has been our warped misguided thoughts that have influenced everything that has happened thus far in our lives. We have the help…if we ask, if we show up and if we commit to changing. If we are hopeless enough, sick enough and worn out enough… we may just give it a try. Let's hope so. It does work…if we work it, there is an AA saying that is right on time for a person ready for recovery. And there is no better place to show up than in the rooms of AA with a group of people who know how you feel, where you are, and what you need to do. The Twelve Step Program started in the rooms of AA and has been working for millions with many addictions. This is a Twelve Step Program that continues to save many lives all over the globe.

As anyone who has been in a Twelve Step Program will tell you that, we all show up with the residuals of alcohol and the Rags that come with it. The Rags were there before we drank, while we drank and are there to haunt us as we become sober. This set of principles in the form of steps, helps us start not only the detox from alcohol but also the detox from what the program calls "Stinking Thinking." These Rags have been with many of us since childhood, then on into adolescence and now they are accompanying us in adulthood.

Fortunately this is not a religious program because many who come in to AA and Twelve Step Programs have no need for a God in their lives, or so they think. With alcoholism comes a great deal of pain and shame. These are two huge Rags of despair that we all need to address, work through, and move away from to a productive, sober and happy life. There does come a time when all of us can look to something greater than ourselves for the help we need. We can call it a tree, a star, a God, the Universe or whatever we need to. There comes a time when there is no doubt that we could ever have hoped to conquer this disease without the help of something bigger and more powerful than we are.

Meetings, meetings, and more meetings will insure the alcoholic or addicted, a better chance at sobriety. Staying sober was never our strong suit. And once we crossed the line into full blown alcoholism, staying sober seemed impossible.

It is the only program to date that really works well. And because of its success with the alcoholic, we can find meetings almost anywhere we go. To look at us as we show up to the world, it is hard to imagine that we were ever isolated, fearful, and lonely drunks with a life of pain.

There are also numbers to call, people to sponsor us. There is love wherever there are meetings because the seasoned AA person will be there to listen and share their similar story. And a drunk sobering up is loved by the group until they can love themselves.

DEPRESSION AND HOPELESSNESS...CAN THEY GO AWAY?
As we start our recovery process, the depression, ups and downs, sick stomach, fearful thinking does not go away easily, but if we are to continue on in our sober living there comes a time when we may even need to seek professional help to aid us in the reasons we are depressed.

The cure is not going to be the drink or a drug that took our life away leaving us in a state of hopelessness. We have come through that if we are abstaining from any mind altering substance. The first drink or drug never stops at one and fails to decrease depression. On the other hand, it adds more depression, and problems, and we find ourselves back in a place even worse than the last time we were living out our addiction. Anyone who slips and slides in and out of sobriety, will tell you it just gets worse. The disease of alcoholism is a disease that will come back with a vengeance if we pick up another drink. Drugs are much the same way as we are not in our right mind with what we are doing and we could overdose, or willfully commit suicide because we are not able to fight off the demons of the depressed state we are in. We definitely are in the Rags of our life again. We may have felt a few of the Riches while we were sober, but they disappear instantly when we return to using drugs and alcohol.

By allowing the depression and hopelessness to rule our lives without the care of a sponsor or attending a series of meetings, we are setting ourselves up. By not talking, calling and showing up to our groups we will slowly slip out of a world that offers us Riches into the Rags and despair of addiction.

The disease of drugs and alcohol is a world that, when not tamed with doing what we need to do in 24-hour tight compartments, one day at a time, will slowly and sometimes quickly come after us in a very subtle way. Cunning is a word that circles the disease of addiction. Our cunning Tiger, sits quietly waiting for us to have a weak moment, to stop doing what we were told to do to stay clean and wants us back.

The DNA that we carry with us is just waiting for the addiction to return. This is a family disease and if we are carrying the disease, we will always be at risk of crossing a line into the world of alcoholism.

And with recovery we find that the only way to stay clean is to take responsibility, seek people who will help and to go to professionals trained in healing our emotional, physical, and spiritual wounds. We, as addicted souls, have lived a life of hiding our diseases. And there are many dis-eases that go with addiction. Maybe the first set of Riches that we get is just recognizing that we have a way out of the lives that are destroying all that we could be. It will take a change.

The question is, do we want to change? Are we willing to change? And will we seek the help we need one day at a time? When we are sober we hear the question a little better than when we are actively participating in our addiction.

The question usually surfaces around our despair; do we want to have the life we are here to live? Is there a Heaven on earth or are we destined to a living Hell? Is there more to this life than just staying sober? Will I lose all my friends? Can I ever dance again or have sex if I am sober? Am I now a dullard?

If we stay fearful we will lose the freedom of recovery. We will never know what we could be or what we could have. Once we have finally admitted that we are hopelessly addicted, we will have a chance one minute and one day at a time as we surrender. We may at first feel surrender is weak but as we continue on we will find it is the strongest, bravest thing we have ever done. When we realize that a power greater than ourselves has our back, we will start to see differently. We will see things we have never seen. In a day of clarity we will see the world of nature, the smiles of children, and a host of other beautiful Riches in our path that we never saw before. And the longer we are sober the more we will see. The life we dreamed about in addiction is the life we now are ready to change our thinking for. We will see a glimpse right away, but not too much because if sobriety were to come easily we would never stay sober.

THE NEXT RIGHT THING IS ALWAYS
THE RIGHT NEXT THING

We are all constantly getting lessons and this is good. We need lessons. We go to school for lessons. We study our lessons to become better with life and on a daily basis life has a great many good lessons to learn from. It may not feel that way at the time, but when we look back we see how we grew, where we were, and where we are now.

The question may arise at some point in one of our life lessons. Are we willing to listen to that still, small voice that lives within us? The voice that is not coming from our chattering head but from a much higher source which manifests through our Heart Chakra. We know when we are in tune with our Higher Self when we are finally able to feel our answers.

We will hear the voice of our Higher Conscious self, nudging us to do the next right thing and then we will get a certain feeling that is free of fear.

DON'T BE A DOUBTING THOMAS
If we are hesitant or doubtful, we will miss that feeling and return to the chatter of our head. But with a head full of chatter, the unhealthy ego disguises the truth by filling us with fear.

We hear many voices that shut out the one small still voice that has our answer. That answer lives with us and within us.

Yet there are times we find ourselves chaotic and full of nothing but fear with nowhere to turn. And of all things, we do not even think to turn within. Instead we find ourselves acting out, full of fear and almost paralyzed, unable to think, let alone move. Oddly enough we forget that the choice of being sick with worry is one that we ourselves choose, either consciously or unconsciously.

We may find ourselves totally withdrawn in silence, and sick with worry or boisterous and demanding, or complacent with no personal commitments to change ourselves. Our ego has us in a choke hold and fills us with chatter that will not allow us to settle down long enough to hear our truth. Yes, that is the answer we always have. It does live within us and we will at some point be so worn down, tired, and limp from our disabling chatter, that we will finally hear a whisper of the answer; an indication that there is an answer and we already know it.

Whenever we stand in fear, we lose our ability to move into action and without action, we are unable to manifest any kind of outcome... good or bad. Even when we are experiencing in-action, this can also be considered action if we are willfully not willing to allow ourselves a change in thinking so that we can change our circumstances.

The life lesson we are attempting to learn can come easily with a surrender or come hard by allowing our stubborn willful side have its way.

The way of the Spiritual Warrior is to surrender to an outdated thinking process and be ready to listen to the next right thing to do. A Doubting

Thomas never has the freedom to leave the pain behind. A Doubting Thomas is more likely to live in the "what ifs" and the "should's" -- the chatter of the unrelenting monkey mind that wants full control of the fear we are manifesting by letting the monkey mind run wild.

Even if we get a glimpse of the truth of what fear is doing to us, we are still in the muck and mire of unimportant fearful thinking until we take the reins of freedom and ride directly into the vapors of Spirit: A God that is waiting for us and has always been there. But we needed to be done with the dark side of fear so that we could see the white light that was a stone's throw away. Fear has no choices. It lives alone. It is responsible for heading us into mindless directions that will ultimately always take us back to the beginning of our current situation until we are willing to take that quantum leap into the light. Fear does not exist until we let it surface. We birth it by the way we allow ourselves to think and we can bury it by the way we change our thinking. This can be done in an instant. But instants are sometimes not enough. It may take minutes, hours or days to consciously change a mindset. But once it has changed, fear will not be allowed back to needle us any longer on the issue we have conquered. The greatest reality takes little hope of such an experience. We will have a better experience the next time the fear monger raises its ugly head. We will have the faith and trust to look back and remember that fear has no control except the control we give it. We can make a decision not to wait as long ever again to let the fear go. Trust is our teacher. Faith and willingness become our friends; these can set us free and do so quickly.

FEAR LOVES TO BE SEDATED BY ADDICTION
A glass of wine or 10. A few beers or a brewery. A bar of chocolate or the whole chocolate factory may still not be enough. A few sleeping pills or narcotics to quiet the mind along with a few shots of vodka or whatever is available. Maybe some weed or crack or cocaine helps silence the fear. But does it? Does it silence the fear or is this the temporary fix that takes all the other body, mind and spirit functions away? When we are addicted to anything, it is true that we have to address the addiction but, as said in the rooms of Twelve Step Programs, addictions are only the tip of the iceberg.

Fear can take us to a place of self-sedation and silence our thoughts. With the addiction of choice, fear will sedate us until fear no longer has power. Our hidden reality that needs to appear is to be willing to step out of fear into freedom. It sounds simple and easy but until we dis-engage our fear, it remains real and a threat to everything we do. There is no clear thinking when fear has stolen our freedom of listening.

Now the real healing begins. Once the addiction is addressed, we find that we have an opportunity to take away the power that fear can hold over us.

The causes, the thoughts, or the person we believe may have caused our addictive behavior is our big cop-out for not taking ownership of our own thinking. We were just trying to forget and wipe out life on life's terms. We tried to silence whatever it was we were not willing to deal with. It has never worked, especially when we wake up to any kind of a sobering moment.

But did that stop us from our great escape into an addiction? Most times not. We kept on trying anyway... hoping for a moment or an hour of peace. We are willing to do anything to distance our thoughts that were driving us insane with constant chatter.

Could it be that the real foundation of our insanity was to not look at what we were running from? Why did we pick an addiction to take us out of our now moments? Was the real insanity that we were just unable and not ready to look and see what was really going on with our lives? Addiction is the foul guy, the scape-goat to ignore our responsibilities to showing up to our lives.

Does an addictive nature work for a while and then stop working? Is there a time when a little of anything was never enough and a lot of everything was never enough either? By letting go and letting the God of our understanding take the reins, we have a chance.

If this is the final resting place for having the opportunity to lose fear, one is sure to know by the hopelessness, and the pain of addiction that causes the loss of friends, jobs, family and possessions.

And then there is the fear factor. That fear that brings us to our knees. If we are ready to change, this will be one of the biggest enlightenments in our life.

It would behoove us to move quickly once we are on our knees and willing to change our thoughts and let our fear exit into the vapors of the Universe. Fear will always want the upper hand and will want us back. But with a Spiritual Warrior suit on, fear cannot penetrate the power of Spirit.

Yes, those addictive behaviors, dangerous, subtle, big or small will want us back. The catacombs of our souls contain not only our answers but have our strength and our power to move forward fearlessly. There is a power greater than ourselves that will feel freedom of life and loss of fearful thinking. This is the enlightened moment when a soul finally knows that it can change to become the person who represents who they really are, not the illusion that has been their prior earthly foot print.

Age, wealth, poverty, social standing in the community are not left out. This is a Yale to Jail experience for all of us. We are in it together in some way or another.

BEING TOTALLY ALIVE MEANS CHANGE: NOW!
The Rags of fear have to go if we get to have a life. And this is not just a letting go process for people with addiction; the Rags of fear exist in all people, in all cultures, in all ways of life. But when it comes to the addicted one, there comes a time when there is no time left. The Rags of fear and addiction, because of fear, must go. Time is up. The fat lady has finished her last song.

Isn't it true that we have always wanted and felt that there were Riches that we could have in this life? We want those Riches even as we sit in the Rags of our addictive life. Somehow, even in our worst moments of fear and addictive behavior we get messages that there is another way to live and we need to live that way NOW.

It may even feel impossible to change. But is not this the head of fear again? How easily it is to be sucked into the vortex of fear. Is trying the answer?

How many times have we tried to change our life circumstances? Is trying the way to go or is trying a lot of work with a bit of failure? What would happen if we stopped trying and started just showing up to a new way of thinking, to create a new way of living?

Have we been so self-absorbed that we have not seen the world around us? There are many who have changed. There are many of us who have been where others have tread; paths that took us out of the world of our own illusions and gave us a life where all things are possible. The Riches are within us.

Being so self-consumed with ourselves and our fears put us into our addictions. The question may arise, how much have I missed? The answer is seemingly unimportant as to what we could have missed had we stayed married to our addiction instead of choosing a marriage with the life we have come here to live. The question that matters is, "Can I return to sanity?" Absolutely screams the Universe! Just knowing that you know where you are in the moment is sanity. The healing has already begun.

CHOICES, CHOICES, CHOICES...AND CHOICES

We may early on in our healing look around and compare ourselves with others, their journey and where they are. Comparisons are very unfair to us and to others. They make our lives seemingly more difficult as if we were a morning bowl of instant oatmeal. We are back to an egoic thought that we want what we want and we want it now.

We are on the planet hopefully for a long time and it takes what it takes to get us where we are going. There is nothing instant about living a full life. Others are doing well and have overcome some of the Rags in their lives by letting go of various forms of addiction and minds full of chatter. They are still in the process of their lives, because as we grow, our lessons are growing with us. We are invited to join a new thought process, a higher conscious state when we are ready. It would be futile to jump ahead of where we need to be. It is a recipe for failure and we eventually need to return to the uncompleted lesson or we will find ourselves in a similar situation.

13

We take our baggage with us. We take our unfinished lessons with us. And this is our choice... that is for sure. No one else can do our lesson or fix us. We are responsible, but we have access to a Power greater than ourselves that will make the journey around the lesson easier. Hopefully we are finally at a point where we are sick enough to want a life free of the Rags and trade them in for a life of Spiritual Riches.

For those of us in the throes of addiction, the disease has a perfect track record to take everything from us and guarantees that if we stay in the insanity of the dis-ease it will give us nothing back.

EMOTIONAL RAGS OR ENLIGHTENMENT

Emotional Rags or enlightenment is the choice we continue to have. We are a soul of elections and the truth of our soul is that we know which one to make. Our job is to learn how to shut down the unhealthy ego so that we can reconnect with the energy that will change our Rags to Riches.

When we have lived with years of baggage, it has been a long walk over a period of time into the forest. We are deep in the forest and the way out will take some navigation. There are many paths and many vines to maneuver. But the forest has served its purpose. We got to hide until it was time to turn around.

There is a well-defined trail to follow to get us to the open meadows where nothing is blinding our vision. We will get a glimpse of our purpose but only a glimpse.

PURPOSE STARTS WHEN WE JUST SHOW UP

There is no searching for our purpose. It lives within us and will surface. We will just know that we know. But to know our purpose is the showing up part. It is the only way to intentionally or unconventionally know that we are being enlightened with personal and important lifetime information.

There is no way to hear new information until we delete all that is no longer serving us. Meditation, prayer, walks in nature, the seaside or any other avenue that quiets us down will help us address the next right thing to do.

Present moment living is the key to hearing the next right thing to do. One step at a time, one day at a time, one moment at a time is the hole in the donut. We cannot have a donut without a hole. So if we are feeling like a hole in the donut, this gives us the substance that is all around us and now it is time to taste the sweetness in life that has been patiently waiting for us. Sound corny? It is cornier to stay disconnected from the donut. In reality, we all need to have the yin and the yang to get where we are going.

Big Ben goes off, our watches chime, and our cell phones play the wake up tune, to remind us that we are now waking up to start living and listening.

WRAPPED UP AND PRESENTED WITH LOVE
The present moment is our biggest gift of the Universe. Will we take this gift with the love that is intended? Are we willing to see our journey in a new way?

If we do, we will experience a rebirth that will change the course of our lives. The present moment is full of real gifts that build real futures without projection. But are we willing to take the risk of living in the now? Is it a risk?

WE ALL GET A RAG OR TWO OR THREE…
Truth-be-told, we all get to experience "Emotional Rags" at certain times in our lives. These Emotional Rags may come in the form of financial challenges, or there may be circumstances that strip away our peace. We could be trapped in our heads and feeling paralyzed. We may be failing in our relationships, or are abandoned by our families. And then, there is always the sadness of losing a loved one.

However, the biggest tiger in the woods is change. We find that change takes us out of our peaceful state and causes us to become paralyzed with fear: unable to think, do or be. But was our peace really a comfort zone or just an illusion of where we thought we were hiding from the reality of our lives? Real peace knows how to face realities.

15

For many of us, change is bigger than death or financial insecurities. In fact, no one is immune to life's "ups and downs," "turns and curves, "stops and starts."

In this regard, our lives are similar to many others along with varying degrees of "ups and downs."

So what is life on life's terms? Is it possible to connect with our higher selves? What if the Grand Prize when dealing with adversities, is doing the right thing? And is there a Grand Prize? What opportunities do we need to seek to discard adversities?

We always know. We have always known. It lives quietly within us. And the good news is that we just have to remember that it is always accessible.

But since we have a human condition, sometimes it takes a trigger, like a disaster or a loss, or health problems to bring us to the knees of our senses. Being forced to slow down, we can finally stop holding our breath and breathe, in a recognized NOW experience. It takes what it takes to catch us off-guard for an on-guard moment. And as is always true, it is in our recognized NOW experience that we will be ready to hear that still small voice that has been patiently waiting for us to tune into.

LIFE IS...AND WILL CHANGE... IT HAS TO

Life IS. Life is always connected to where we are in our thinking and then living experience. The truth of our spiritual essence -- the real us -- is always with us whether we are in good or challenging situations. Our souls are the real thing, the real us. As for our minds, when we become mindful on a soul level we are clearly connected to a Power greater than ourselves. We can attest to that by noting our decisions and their outcome.

When life is solely manifesting on life's terms without a connection to our spiritual side, it places us in the trenches of despair, addiction, fear, and feeling useless. There is always an open road to our Spiritual Riches but it does require us to change our thinking and then be willing to connect to something that may feel familiar.

We may feel that the discomfort we have been living with is normal and hence will keep us locked up in the despair. Without being willing to change our situation, our God-given spiritual nature will lie dormant. The second we let some light in from our Source and Supply and recognize the power that lives within us, we will at that time change our adverse experiences.

Despair is the emotional rag that calls up opportunities to guide us to the changes we need to proceed to a better, more purpose-fulfilled life.

Gratitude becomes something we start to feel in all situations, especially the ones that are seemingly turning around.

In the throes of despair, we may not want to feel very grateful but without recognizing despair, we would not be able to address the challenge. So gratitude could be referred to as the yin that needs the yang. The yang cannot happen without the yin. Just as despair has its opposite of a healing agent, we get to observe that in any thought process there is an opposite, another side that actually can complement the learning process. We cannot learn without the complement of opportunity when we are in despair. Some may refer to this as a wake-up catch-all; or just a wake-up call.

This so called wake-up call usually comes at a point in our lives when we are deeply in trouble. We feel abandoned, fearful, and depressed as our life is not going our way. The other side of the coin is when we hear a voice that tells us that we may well be a "soul" of substance and purity, and a "soul" of many choices. Not what we expected to hear and usually not what we want to hear. We are too far gone and that is when desperation conjurers up a call for self-healing.

Is our soul begging to be heard? Or are we begging to let it out of the closeted state of discontent? So we wonder, what are our choices? Why are we here anyway? This is when we may toy with suicidal thoughts as an additive to our on-going drama. But is this not another gratitude moment in disguise?

Could it be that we are worn out from all the chatter in our heads and we have nowhere to turn...but do we? We are in the state of what some refer to as "the quantum leap". We are sort of ready to jump into a new life but afraid. We want more. We need more. But how could a change in thinking and a quantum leap be of value to us? After all we have been this way all our lives. We have been with our chatter bypassing our soulful messages for a long time. But hope does return even to the most disconnected and disenchanted. The soul is alive and is already connected to something greater than ourselves. We just missed the miracle. We were too busy being self- absorbed, selfish with our addictive natures, and unaware of anybody else around us. We may have pretended to care...but did we or were we just good at pretending to listen and pretending to care?

Time comes around and lets us know that the old way no longer works. It shadows us with reminders and gives us daydreams of what could be. With all the self- effort in the world, we try to leave the controlling ego that has convinced our minds not to listen. We soon realize we need help. We need help from something bigger than ourselves. And we then must prepare to go to our Source and Supply with our request. A full surrender is needed. A return to sanity comes. And in the third step of AA we read that we must turn our will and our lives over to the care of God. Who wants to really do that? We love the control. We want the control and cannot imagine giving it up. But only if we are fortunate to realize that our control only means we are out of control, will we get the healing vapors of Spirit, our Guides and our Angels to see us through.

WAKE UP OR KEEP THE NIGHTMARE GOING

We may not always take the opportunity to listen and change, as our egos still love to hold on to control, especially through all the fear messages that are popping through our brains on a regular basis. With years of turmoil and addictive behaviors the ego seems very powerful at convincing us that we have all the answers.

And, we do. But not from the chattering ego that brings us messages from the past and future that plays into our doubting, self-loathing fears.

Somehow in all the chatter, there are messages trying to surface that are there for our greater good. We will continue to receive messages that feel "right." But will we hear them?

If we do, the waking to our lives has started. Once the messages are re-occurring we will want to decipher what has caused us to wake up at this time, and what is our next right thought needs to continue hearing the messages that are meant for our best interest.

Remembering that Emotional Rags serve a purpose and are the vehicles to receiving our Spiritual Riches the Rags take on another life and are ready to exit. There is work to do but they are at the starting line and know that they have been beaten. They know that they cannot stay the same anymore. Their life is up as the old ways are no longer working. By letting go of our Emotional Rags, we are ready to start getting a glimpse of our intended Riches. We are going to have the answers we need through listening and to know how to manifest our deepest desires. The desires of the heart that are meant to be shared with humanity are ready to be shared. If we so choose not to take this time to manifest our intended journey, it may be life times before the opportunity on such a grand scale shall arise again.

In a state of peaked awareness, we will gain a realization that there is a significant difference between chattering egos and the deep warm knowing that we know, and it comes with clarity from our hearts.

We begin to realize that in our state of awareness it is time to consider making better decisions. We want to start thinking differently. But can we? Will we? Even with good intentions, unless we are ready to move out of our Emotional Rags, we will have little reprieve, if any, from our old way of thinking.

There too, for some of us, is a determination that we can go it alone. We try to make life happen on our own terms. We were taught to pull up our bootstraps and get going. It may work for a short time but if addiction is in our lives, the success rate is almost nil.

For those who do tough it out, they are usually living a dry drunk, resentful that they cannot successfully have their addictions. If a major disaster happens in their lives, a return to addiction is a common choice to alleviate the pain. And of course, the pain gets worse with a return to substance abuse.

There is a way to live successfully and happily with an addiction to drugs and alcohol. But the successful way is not by going it alone. We have help. We have a choice and a voice. Turning to the God of our understanding puts us in direct connection for protection. Centering and remembering that we are ready for a new life is helpful, too. One day at a time. One second at a time. If we live in the NOW and stay present to our surrender and our protection from something greater than ourselves, we are safe. If we start getting squirrely, we call someone or we go to an AA meeting. What we do not do is sit in our pity and not show up to our next right thing. The choice to show up is the choice to have the life we know belongs to us.

What if we are willing to forfeit valuable help from our Higher Power and we start to listen to the unhealthy ego with all its "shoulds" and "what ifs"? That is not the way of our soulful warrior.

The ego in this instance is not our friend. It wants us back. Returning to our past, even for a moment and finding that we think it will be different this time, means that the ego has won again and we have lost. The chatter of the ego is ruling our lives yet again and we are in deep trouble.

At first we may feel like we have a handle on our addictions. We may feel strong and consumed with the message that it will be different this time. We become like a run-a-way freight train. We are destroying everything in our path including ourselves. We are back to the same old, same old life in an instant of insanity. Self-will run riot is the formula that fails. We have lost our way and the Emotional Rags have returned with a vengeance. There are no Riches to be found. The healthy messages are gone. We are unable to connect to our Higher Self. We are exactly where we should be and need to be; in the gutter of our life. And each time we go there it becomes harder and harder to retrieve our mindfulness, our health and our connection to Spirit.

We forget that the universe is friendly, kind, and ready to be a help to us and our Rags are susceptible to Riches. When will we finally let go to let this play out in our favor? Again, the decision is always ours.

FEAR MOTIVATOR OR A LOSS OF FREEDOM?

Fear at times can motivate us. Run to safety! Stay away from the Tiger... head for cover, there is a tornado coming! Fear definitely has a role in our lives when it comes to staying attuned to dangerous situations.

Does fear really exist in our emotional drama or do we make it up as we go? Are others able to steal our energy and make us fearful? What can we do to not buy into the self-made movie of fear? First of all, we need to know that emotional fear caused by ourselves or others is not true until we make it true.

It is once again a valuable lesson in learning to turn our attention to something greater than ourselves. In a fearful state we can see that we have separated ourselves from a loving God and a loving Universe. Who really would do that with intention? Most of us are not even aware that we are living with fear. We have become accustomed to how it feels. We may want the peace that seems to be lacking, but we are not equating loss of peace with fear.

Fear used incorrectly can be a total loss of freedom and a tool of the ego keeping us locked out of our heart center; the real message center. The original purpose of fear has become more than a voice of rescue. Fear has actually evolved and partnered with our ego to scare us from living our lives to the fullest potential. Fear takes away the freedom of co-creating with the God of our understanding. It is an energy that wants to work with us.

It is healthy to understand that sometimes Emotional Rags are caused by fear. Our Emotional Rags continue to multiply until we change the way we think. Our thoughts encourage the "good" and "bad" in our lives. If Emotional Rags are laced with fearful decisions that prevent us from moving forward, we are sacrificing our Spiritual Riches. Our Riches cannot infiltrate our lives when we are living in fear.

Have we ever stopped long enough to contemplate our own story of the Emotional Rags that are holding us back? *What does our fear sound and look like? Are we even able to recognize it, or are we so used to "fearful living" that fear has become second nature to us?*

Fear IS. Fear IS, just as Peace IS. When we are in fear…it is recognizing the relentless chatter of our egos and we are listening. When we are in peace… we are recognizing calmness in the heart. We are thinking with clarity.

WE ARE WRITING OUR OWN STORY
There comes a time for all of us that we are stopped in our tracks. Something happens that wakes us up.

We become aware of our own story. Why does this happen and why is this necessary? We realize that we are living the way we have been thinking. We either want to keep our present lives, or we are willing to change them.

Our story could have a happy ending but is laced with fear and that becomes the story we are currently living. We know that we are *fearful*. We know that we want to dispel the fear. But are we willing to release it to something bigger and greater than ourselves?

Almost everyone will agree that there is something bigger than we. Once recognized, the fog lifts, and our mask is removed. The answers show up clear and crisp. Releasing fear is in itself a spiritual richness. We will feel a peace and feel it immediately. We stop holding our breath waiting for the next shoe to drop. Most of us have not realized that most of us hold our stress breath for long periods of time. We are actually holding our breath. There is no true inhale and exhale. We are living like a stalled vehicle on a busy freeway. We need our gas back.

Spiritual Riches explode once the Rags are exposed and the change is truly one we desire. It is a time of rebirthing and we well may do the cleansing of rebirthing many times in this lifetime. Once we have been introduced and tempted, with such wonderful life gifts, we can never successfully go back to the old way our lives once were. Some of us will stay the same but the seeker never has peace once life has been shown with all its possibilities and all its Riches. It still is a choice and some of us will fear change and others will take the leap and embrace the moment. We may have this. It remains in our powerful control. Piloting our course is the way of the Spiritual Warrior.

Even though fear sometimes lurks in a secret disguise, once exposed we must take on a stealthy attitude of transparency and look at the fear squarely in the face. If we are noticing and feeling that the fear wants to own us and take away our freedom of thought, we will feel elation the moment we recognize the Tiger in the woods. Pet the Tiger, love the woods, and dispense with a chattering EGO that wants to take away the gift on which we are about to embark. Our once obsessive EGOS now have a different kind of power over us, the spiritual power that blocks the fear, and we proceed by letting go and letting the Universe have the first move. It is always helpful to remember that "letting go" creates the change that prompts us to jump back in the ring of life. All we need to do is take an action step of listening. In that initial moment of acceptance it is good to move quickly from our heart center and remember that "change is change only." Change will always be a constant in our lives in our Now and Forevermore. Change has to keep changing or we would no longer be alive. As we look back at change, we will notice that we grow spiritually and, we will see why it was needed.

CHOICES OF ADVERSITY OR FEAR OF CHANGE

Once we are in that mode of making a choice, we can accept adversity. We actually need to if we are going to move away from adversity. In our moment of choice we either return to our fearful self or seek the opportunities looming in front of us. Because we have a choice, it will begin to feel less risky. There will be no risk in changing because again we will remember that "change" is always a part of our lives, like it or not. "Change" is not even the calculated risk we may once have thought it was.

Once we embrace change we have embraced the IS of our lives. We are on to the discovery of Spiritual Gifts.

ACCEPTANCE IS THE KEY TO CHANGE

The quicker we accept opportunities to "change," the quicker we are able to do what we need to do. We will stop putting our lives on hold, and fighting the inevitable.

It could be that acceptance of change is a lot to swallow and it will be until we wrap our heads and heart around the fact that the only way to personal freedom will be through the acceptance of change. But this time, if we accept that we have the power needed over change, we will know that we are not and never have been alone. In the end we will just be the change.

But, what happens when we are just not ready to embrace major changes? We can fight it for a while. We can ignore it for a time. Hiding from a needed change can be brutal but we have all done it at one time or another. When we are sick and tired of being sick and tired regarding what we need to do…we will get the kick in the pants, the knock on the head, the bad cold or flu or maybe even a broken bone. We will be slowed down to re-evaluate. Anyone that has come down with a sickness can relate to knowing that they needed to stop, slow down and listen. Change was needed and change was in the air and finally by being stopped we get to access the reasons, listen to the whys and then get into contact with our still small voice that will give us the reasons for the change and how to walk through it. We can't fight it, or try to leave it. But we can agonize on why we will not take the change needed. Fortunately we are not judged harshly by a loving Universe. The God of our childhood has been exposed to being kind, loving and ready to help us when we are ready to receive. There is a missed opportunity, at the time we have been nudged to act. However, we will intuitively, deep in our soul, know and feel that we have somehow missed out on an opportunity and this feeling does not leave us; and if it does comes back later in our lives, it is in the form of regrets.

THE SOULFUL US ALWAYS KNOWS THAT WE KNOW

The soul houses all activity of the heart. If we have regrets, in our present NOW moments, for not accomplishing what we could have accomplished, we will find that our lesson many times will appear again in front of us. The next opportunity may be harder, take longer, and need more time. The Universe was ready for us at one time. But by waiting, there will need to be another alignment put into place to accomplish the change we initially could have had in a much easier way. It cannot be said enough that a loving PRESENCE in the Universe does not judge our ability or inability to change - but we do. As most of us know, self-judgments are extremely hard because human conditions missed take a longer self-process to forgive. Most of us want to show up to the ALL in our lives. And everyone's considered ALL does vary according to the way we think. We may need more time and we will always get the time we need to walk through more life experiences that will help us evolve to that level of trust in something we can feel but not see. Noticeable and acceptable change is a way to our Spiritual Riches. We start to learn, and recognize what is or is not working for us. This is a sure way to be in a mode for accepting the Spiritual Riches that are starting to show up. We are then prepared, and ready to live in our NOW fully, thus not missing out on our next right thing to do as we have started to learn how to accept the precious gifts of change.

We start showing up fully to the life we are here to live. *We feel good. We have purpose because we are the purpose in all that we do.* We are not stagnating. Rather we listen for our next move into that nirvana state that will peacefully guide us into an arena of peaceful knowledge. We may even sometimes wonder why we stayed so connected to the fear of change for so long. It just takes what it takes. The ego will stutter and shake and lose power.

Once our ego has lost power, we begin to *almost welcome change*. And so it goes that with the loss of fear comes an automatic "richness of faith." Many times we do not even realize how connected we are to faith.

We do start to feel that there is another way to finding our way. Faith and trust present themselves and even at the tail end of addictive living we somehow can feel a great deal of loving presence around us. That is what faith is and does in our mindless absence. It shows up in another person talking to us or we find it talking to us in a moment of silence.

More specifically, once we accept the fact that faith has a shadow the surly chattering ego cannot live long disrupting our healthy emotions when we have faith.

Being addictive in nature and listening only to our fearful self, it will take Emotional Rags for us to find a way to experience the faith that is needed to catapult us into Spiritual Riches. Let us face it...we are not going to go to a concept of faith if everything is going okay or we think it is going okay.

It is a ride of a lifetime but not one to be missed. Once on that up-hill roller coaster, going over the first plunge is no longer that bad. Faith has become our seat belt. It is snug and tight around us. We are ready for the rest of the ride.

There has been much talk as to how to have things, how to get stuff, how to have more. Even Spiritual books have been written about the way to get more. But is getting more stuff real abundance? Is having unlimited money securing our future? Or are we securing stuff and money so that we look affluent and abundant?

Abundance has to embrace all life categories for us to feel and say that we are experiencing abundance. What are these categories?

How are our peace, our intentions? How about our resentments, judgments, and basic moral code? Are we really abundant or just getting by, even when our pockets are full of money. There have been many self-help books written on how to get money. But what is the passion that will bring us our money and then distribute it with clarity, responsibility, and good judgment? Will we have peace and joy? Will we be truly content? What is the level of abundance we are looking for? And most importantly will it ever be enough? Those answers live within us. Money will not fix addictions. Money is not the answer to happiness. Money is not evil. Money is money. We need it to survive and to have the things that make us happy. The big picture for abundant living is having it all and that means having more than just money to be living in the style we privately request from our Source and Supply.

MONEY MAKES THE WORLD GO AROUND

We need it and that should not make us feel guilty or evil for wanting it. If we were paying our way in apples, we would need our orchards of apples to get us what we need.

Having and using and enjoying money does not have to be our life story. If we are living in lack, money can trigger fear - fear of not having our needs met, or not having our needs met enough. And if we are spending our money without a sense of respect, like using our money to feed an addiction, any addiction, we will find ourselves not having enough.

There are even some millionaires who live in fear of losing their money. Money seems to define them and without it they may feel a loss of identity. So we all can have issues with money if we do not take time to change our thinking on what money really is and how it weaves into the rest of our life. People have committed suicide because they lost their money. People have drunk themselves to death over money.

In the 1930's, when the Stock Market crashed, people were jumping out of windows. In recent times, people died stressful deaths in the early 2000's, because their stocks dropped to nothing in a sinking economy. It was a temporary problem but not for those who took their lives thinking that they would not have enough.

The question arises, "*Will we ever have 'enough,' and will we ever be happy and content with what we have? Or… does more stimulate the need for more?*" Can this fearful addictive thinking cause us to have an emotional rag around money while not addressing the things that need to be healed that are around money and connected to money. Letting go of money and the worry around it brings more money. As in all things, letting go is the answer to having it all.

RELATIONSHIPS ARE IN EVERYTHING, $ TOO

When we move on, whether it is with a person or money, our relationships start to change. They heal and move on or stay the same. Once again, we are faced with some choices. The "high road" of healthy letting go and moving on is one of the hardest moments. And it is our easiest road to recovery.

Without living in a letting go and letting God world, this process can be extremely difficult until we get the hang of it. It works, but we need to give it a try. Trying the letting go process in small things gives us an opportunity to see how this process works. There may be a fearful moment where we think that by letting go we are losing control. And we are. And we need to if we want to manifest a good outcome. We may find ourselves asking in desperation, "What is it going to be like?" "What if I never have companionship again?" "What if my sister never talks to me for the rest of my life?" This is when the over-active ego creeps in and would like to rape us of our chance to have closure on anything that we need to address. We are finding ourselves without the opportunity for new beginnings. So we fall back into a familiar pattern where we do not get what we wish for. What a good time to stay on *the high watch. The opportunity looms before us and never goes away. We go away but can come back. Letting go of the fear and embracing faith, is a life changer totally letting us have all the abundance we can handle. What a good time not to lose faith in the process of change and the life it has to offer.* It is totally up to us!

THE PRESENTING-SELF NEEDS AUTHENTICITY

The presenting-self has a big job if it is not authentic. It wants everyone to like us, love us and not question who and what we stand for. Usually we are standing for whatever we think someone else wants to hear so that we fit in. This is the non-authentic side of the presenting-self. It can also be a tool that we use to push others away so that they cannot detect addictive behavior or the low self-esteem we live with on a daily basis.

On the other end of the spectrum is the authentic-self that is not afraid to be transparent. We are the souls that have nothing to lose and nothing to hide by telling our story as it really is. All the ups, and downs, the dreams, the lost and found, the lives of others touched and revealed in our own experience.

When we are truly authentic and transparent, we are free. However, here are some of the old questions that we are faced with when we find ourselves making up our story as we go. *What will people think if they know who I really am? What do they already know about me? Or think they know? What do I need to hide?* It takes a great deal of energy to hide who we really are. We are always on over-time with the job to not only come up with a story we think others want to hear but then we have to remember what we said for future reference.

At some point we all have an opportunity to change the way we do our personal communication. Our old way of thinking and living becomes outdated once we get the nudge that it no longer is working for us. The addictions that bring us to our knees become the opening to standing tall with a new way of thinking and living. We begin to co-create with something bigger than ourselves, and come to know that whatever we need, with the highest of intentions, will come to us easily and on time. The journey has shifted and it feels right.

OOPS, A SLIP...WHAT TO DO NOW?

We take our new information and give it a try and all of a sudden, we have slipped. We may have slipped with a drug, or we may have slipped with the way we are thinking but it is a slip and we are feeling the pain. If there was no fear, it comes anyway. We feel overwhelmed, guilty and depressed. We failed! But did we really fail yet or are we learning how to negotiate and listen to our deeper self? Does the connected self have our best answers? Recognizing a slip is a form of healing. Ignoring the slip means most often that we are not ready to make the necessary commitments. We are still living in our Emotional Rags. The next right thing is rather simple and it does work. After a slip, if we pick up where we left off, we have not lost much ground and we have learned a great deal about losing touch with our inner guide. It may well be that we were compulsively busy, lost in a resentment, or questioning whether or not we have a real problem with a substance or thinking pattern.

We think it will take an act of Providence for us to change our thinking patterns. We may have thought that we had but find that we have not. An act of Providence is the help we need to listen for. By not giving in to the slip, and picking up our new life right where we left off, is a sure way to return to sanity and the ongoing road of recovering. Recovering is a rebirth. We all do it. We all have slips. But souls that are willing to note the issue that took us out of our healing zone, are the ones that have not lost their recovery mode. At this time in a healing state, we have already learned a great deal and with a slip we are learning more about what triggers us and what we need to do in the event that we are feeling ourselves losing the conscious contact with our Higher Power.

If we choose to not pick up where we left off, we will find ourselves regressing and hopeless once again.

We find we are the image we have created in our own mirror. We know 'way too much and it becomes haunting for us to not stick with our quest for Spiritual Riches. It is all good. Mistakes give us information. We need the journey we are on to not leave anything out. And it will not.

WHAT'S AN ENLIGHTENED SOUL TO DO?
We start getting flooded with self-questioning. There are a lot of questions and we need to choose if we are willing to answer them.

Do we want to stay where we are, or listen to what our heart has been nudging us with? If finances are the primary concern and a fearful self-stopper, trust in our process has been lost. We may not even be aware of losing trust. We may still have it but for some reason we cannot identify the voice that lives within us that is our real champion. Fear now has become our life story. That is for the moment until we come to our senses. There is an obsession that sets in telling us from our fearful ego that we do not have enough and worse yet, we never will have enough. If we believe this about finances, we can look across the board of our life and notice that we believe that about everything. When things are good we often do not even realize it. There seems to be that left shoe ready to always drop with potential future loss.

It does not occur to us that the future is still the future. We stay in our own movie of drama, despair, and victim-hood to some degree or another.

The story of gloom and doom and fear is the way we are accustomed to living and seems quite natural. We have been scared for a long time by the evil twin of fear which keeps our Divine Purpose from unfolding. The Tiger will need to get out of the cage if it wants to have its freedom.

So what is a troubled yet enlightened soul to do? Change our thinking is the only option that will work. How do we do that? There are many ways to change our thinking and there is one way that is well suited for all of us. It is a way that we have always had that lives within us and now it is time to access our Spiritual Power and start the process of making our changes to become the soul we really have always been and are now.

Being faced with old thoughts attempting to keep us in our past of Emotional Rags and emotional drama, is a normal event that comes and goes. Living with fearful old thoughts that contain their brothers and sisters of resentment, along with many other ways that we used to think, are not ready to leave quickly. They have been with us a long time. But there is a way to find another home for them; one that lives galaxies away.

There are always going to be times in our lives when emotional situations, such as a loss of money, a job, a relationship, friends or family discord, remain in the forefront of our minds. Our human side needs this to grow. But with a change in thinking, we will not stay connected for long. As we grow to love peace more than chaotic, egoic thinking, we will find ourselves resolving many of our challenges much more quickly.

THE GAGGLE OF CHATTER NEEDS TO GO

We are having a great day and moving through it with ease...until out of the blue we get a knock-down, drag-out experience that we had no clue was coming our way. The egoic "mind chatter" is on a rampage. The courtyard is full of unwanted voices and that seems to be all that we can hear. A lot of nothing that seems so important is coming through like a sieve. We may feel that we cannot fight our chattering perpetrators. The gaggle of chattering monkeys has a hold of our minds, and refuses to let up, or so we may think. They are releasable but first we have to know that we are being ambushed and next that we can send these monkeys away.

How? How do we send the chattering gaggle of monkeys away? First we have to admit to ourselves that they are not real and what they have to say is not real either. Then we have to remember that we are addicted to these messages most of the time because we seem to feed on the fear they are sending. Saying out loud that they are dismissed is a wonderful way of hearing ourselves issue a command that will instantly silence these perpetrators. They cannot have our power unless we give them the power to control our thoughts. Retuning to our NOW and to doing the next right thing is the gift that we all have to return to sanity. Addiction has many arms and if we are an addictive person, we are easily trapped by the octopus grabbing our attention, holding us tightly, and squeezing the life out of us. Switching addictions, simply put, means becoming obsessed with anything other than our present moment. We are always allowed to stay in the "yets" of what we need to do to come to our senses. But the proven way to success is "letting up, letting go" and letting your Higher Power take the reins. Try it. It is a nice ride. There is a voice that will come to us full of love and guidance when we are finally ready to listen. It is a clear Universal, God-given voice that lives within all of us that is prepared to battle an out-of-control ego. This is the God-Centered voice of the heart that the ego cannot touch. Should you have a problem with the word God, pick something greater than yourself and you will have the same result.

LISTENING OR CHATTER? A CLEAR CHOICE

The chance to exercise the power of listening is magical. We can learn to be observers of the good messages that come through our soulful heart center or not.

We can even casually look on at the ego and its misfit messages, and observe the chatter as if it were a Board of Directors out of control in a meeting we never even called. To observe could be considered an action step where we quietly look on without participating. We may even want to compare our observations in the same vein as watching a sports event. We are looking at decisions of what may happen. Our head becomes full of assumptions as we are trying to think it through as if we could call the play that would win the game. The ego of monkey-mind chatter has the answers that we want to hear. But are these real answers or assumptions of an out-come? If we are caught off guard, and are accidentally quiet for a moment or two, our heart center could pop in to be heard with not an observation but the truth of what we are seeing play out. In this moment we will be able to make clear, concise decisions. Our heart center steps to the plate. The truth is revealed. This practice, once learned, is always the next "right" thing to do. The clarity of our bountiful supply of Spiritual Riches is now available during our present moments.

THE HEART ALWAYS KNOWS TO KNOW
When we are ready to grow, a positive message of the heart will always appear. That still small voice within us has been working overtime to get our attention in between all the chatter. There was nobody home. We were not really there. We just could not hear the messages. However, the real voice that has our answers fortunately does not give up. The voice of the heart can come through in small increments of messages or one big loud… "HEY YOU!" When we are in a growth spurt spiritually, we are bombarded with attention- getting messages until we finally hear them.

FINDING OUR HEART ONLY HAPPENS IN THE NOW
Living in the NOW, and finding our authenticity and transparency are two important tools that will help us in the showing up process that gives us our freedom to grow and access to a talking informative heart.

Because we are learning that "Change" is eminent, and even if we are in the throes of depression, anger, or fear, we still will have opportunities to access our heart center, when at times it comes through in our subconscious. Our NOWS are now and we can learn to see them as they are. Living in the NOW helps not only see what is happening in our present situation but also in building a future. When we are not projecting a false future, our NOW is creating the story and that story is so much better than the one we dramatized.

The Universe is a very powerful Source and Supply and will always await our recognition no matter how long it takes. We get to be ready when we are ready. Because there is no separation from the God of our understanding unless we choose, we can access the ONENESS that gives us our power to now know that all things we do, think or become, are part of that Source and Supply that has always been available to us. Once we resist separation, we realize the "ONENESS" in all things we have come to know and be the truth.

NUDGES CAN TICKLE THE COCKLES OF YOUR HEART
We will get nudges in our lives. These nudges give us another source of information and the guidance that will help us live our lives guided by what we are really here to learn and where our purpose best suits the greater good of all. This is the beginning of truly showing up to our lives.

Spiritual Riches co-exist with us. They are always around us and always have been. Many of us are just too busy with fast living and over-active chattering egos to know how close our happiness really is.

Riches come in many faces. We are rich when we see nature in all her glory. We see this beauty as soon as we start the process of deleting our Emotional Rags. And interestingly enough, once we start to notice the natural beauty around us, we are no longer in the drama of an emotional rag, one that has kept us locked up in the fear of not knowing what we think we already know or need to know.

THE SQUIRM THAT LIVES WITHIN
Spiritual Riches tend to jump up and down, wiggle and squirm deep within us. This is the way the Emotional Rags try and escape the grips of our unhealthy ego. We constantly get a glimpse of Spiritual Richness whether we realize it or not. If we only took a breath in the middle of our busy minds and busy days obsessively trying to get everything done, we would sense that there is a message coming through. And this message is clear, to the point, and full of solutions to anything that we may think is a challenge or unobtainable. When the Spiritual Riches knock at our door, *will you let yours in? Don't worry, they will keep on knocking.*

It takes a great deal of spiritual bravery to surrender our old ways of thinking. Bravery comes in the form of being mindful and willing to do what we need to do without a lot of questioning and trust. We may have had years of thinking in a negative fearful way. Even though it has never worked, we can still feel at a loss as to how we can change. We are so used to our thinking that we keep on thinking the way we always have and for some insane reason, we think this is normal.

Changing our thinking will change and save our lives. We will know little sickness, low doses of fear, and our resentments will fade and our relationships will prosper because we are no longer living in reactive judgment.

When our thinking has changed and we are discarding all the old behaviors that no longer work, we will become available to the guidance of this majestic Universe, which is the God of our understanding in full glory. There will no longer be ways that we come up with to go back to that old way of living without enormous discomfort. The discomfort will be different than the discomfort we have with all our life problems that keep eating away at us. Those problems will be gone and in order to get them back it will take more work than the work we did to change our thinking and change our lives. If "born again" is in our lingo, then this is the real born again results for us. We are new, the past is gone, the future holds hope and we have mindfulness in the present moment.

EMOTIONAL RAGS STIR UP OPPORTUNITY
Oddly enough, Emotional Rags are the catalyst to Spiritual Riches. *Who would have guessed it could be so straightforward? Why me Lord...Why Me?* And then there is the, *"Why not me?"* We will never know the multitudes of light beams around us until we know our darkness. But the minute the light beam on anything shines through, darkness dissipates quickly.

The "yin and yang" of a life have purpose. *So, what are those purposes? First things first, is to acknowledge that we want to live in the light. The light has our answers and has our life purpose well- displayed as it comes through our consciousness. Once we are living with good intention, we are living our life*

35

purpose and it is at this point that our life purpose grows. Living addictively hides our light.

IDENTIFYING EMOTIONAL RAGS

One of the first identifiable signs of being in an emotional rag is that we feel off kilter, and our energy is zapped. We are constantly thinking, thinking, thinking. We cannot get the voices out of our head. Our energy is so compromised that we at times are not motivated to do anything let alone address an addiction problem or any problem that is feeding on our emotions. At this stage of feeling there usually is no idea of what Riches we could have by addressing these nagging Emotional Rags. Success, prosperity, and peaceful living will elude us until we address the Rags that are pushing us to make better decisions or just telling us to get off our butts and show up. If we have learned that our healing answers live within us, we are ready to start the process of listening. The Riches are awaiting us. We just need to do our start-up and use the tools to get us focused and listen to our hearts for clear cut direction.

The quest we are on is to be aware through our adversities. Opportunities will come forward with our due diligence. If we have been living in separation from all life including our own, we will not be able to tap into the oneness that lives all around us and in us. And if we *are living in separation, we will find that we have isolated ourselves from all sources that are waiting to guide us out of our Emotional Rags. Then who can possibly help us? Who will possibly care about what we need?* Our energy becomes stagnant, our light dims, and we find we have little interest in anything except how to make ourselves feel better. This is a time when many will turn to addictive living. They will find ways to medicate themselves with drugs, alcohol, food, sex, gambling or a host of other obsessive behaviors so that they do not have to address their life's solutions. This is not the answer to solving an emotional rag. But sometimes what it takes for some of us is to bottom- out to get our attention.

It may be time to take a deep breath and breathe in the God of our understanding. Have we bottomed out or do we see where we could? Can we catch ourselves before we lose, hurt, or kill someone? What will it take?

BREATHING IN A BREAKTHROUGH

It very well may be the time to take a moment and look at where we are. What is our immediate now looking like? Are we ready to accept a breakthrough or are we going to be status quo for a while longer and keep doing and thinking the way we have been?

Our NOW moment could turn out to be one more opportunity that many of us fail to recognize. We could be at a turning point. But are we not all connected in some form or another? The ego wants nothing to do with ONENESS. Our unhealthy egos are far too selfish. But once we recognize that separation is not the truth of who we are, the ego's power over us diminishes. But don't be fooled, it is not gone. It hibernates. It patiently waits for us to resume a selfish oneness approach to living. It opens us to addictive thinking and medicating to shut down the chatter of the ego. But the ego has won again. We are back to doing what we do to get the same old results. Back we go into separation, unavailable to the gift of Oneness and the Spiritual Riches of the heart that continue to wait for us. We are all separate again.

FORGET THE TREASURE HUNT-IT'S IN US

It does not take a treasure hunt to realize that the treasure is not hidden from us, just eluding us. The treasure will appear once we trust that it is there. This will be the act of faith that it takes to uncover something that has been with us all along. But until we are ready to accept it, the treasure remains stealth.

THERE ARE NO HIDDEN CLUES TO WIN

We will get many clues and nudges, and sometimes we will also get nagged; we may even feel broken. But if we leave our Senior Partner, the God of our understanding, we just need to remember that we left and Spirit did not. Our Riches are there for us. They are there. They have always been there. They will appear as soon as that emotional rag we have been carrying around has been deleted from our consciousness by a willing surrender. We can always ask, *"Where are they?"* And, by listening to the still, small voice that lives within all of us, we will get our answer. The Universe never misses a question, a phone call, a test, or request. It could be almost comical to think that we get our answers when we show up to our daily lives and the devices we use for communication. Why would God or the Universe call us? Why not? Does not the God of all live and breathe in everything? God talks. It may be through our next friend or even a stranger. In an addictive state, we would never be available for the answers and the way they come through. We are not available to anything including ourselves.

Once we have surrendered to the fact that we can find our spiritual treasures, we will find that the hunt can be exciting and full of surprises. We are seeing differently. We are feeling differently and can now access the present moment. We are in it and we know it. *A present moment experience in the NOW is an awesome enlightening experience. We are experiencing a major shift in consciousness. Change in thinking has set in. There is an acceptance of having what we thought was not ours and it comes through clearly in the way we are thinking.* In this reality moment, we are showered with the richness of just knowing that we have finally moved into a new dimension. We are one with the Universe and we will see things we never saw before. We will see that nothing is hidden from us. We were hiding from our gifts. That has now changed.

Listening becomes natural. We are ready to let go of old antiquated ideas that we picked up through old out-dated learned behaviors or stubbornness that we picked up along our way. Our pasts have faded away. Our futures intuitively hold promise if we build them in our now. Yes, we now know that we are connected. A new sense of freedom sets in.

Showing up to the hunt is the only way to find the information needed to experience a full revelation to acquire our Spiritual Riches. With all that we have done to gain these Riches, we will see that our thinking has kept us floundering. Our Spiritual Riches have never been in hiding and have always been in our line of sight. We just were blinded by old thinking. We were blinded by unhealthy egos, and old thought patterns that fight with our heart center.

It is always in our best interest to remember how devious and cunning our ego is. An ego is a rag that is willing to halt discoveries on the path to Spiritual Riches. Egos cannot stand up to truth and fear, or authentic NOW thinking patterns. The ego retreats quickly. But, do not be fooled, the ego patiently awaits opportunities to trigger fearful conversations in our head. It often feels like we have been ambushed.

IS THERE A PLAN...OR ARE WE THE PLAN?
A path to Spiritual Riches needs a plan, and most importantly, it needs a "willingness" to search for the treasure by moving in the next right direction.

Truthfully, some may find that their lives are somewhat of a train wreck. Staying away from our destinations because we have been in a wreck is not an invitation to never board life again. And there is no promise that we will never be in a train wreck in our life again. Getting off the train of life, and never boarding our next leg in our journey doesn't work either.

We need to re-board our next train and the next, only this time with a new way of thinking: *a life train that is going somewhere more suited for us. It usually is the one we always knew we should be on but we were afraid that we were wrong.*

Our new destination is calling us. Let it.

So why not climb back on the next train, and get started with a journey of the intuitive heart. One that has been calling and hounding us for a long time. It appears as a natural feeling to take an in-depth look at where we are, what we are doing, and where we want to go.

It is also natural to accidentally by-pass something that we are well suited for on this incredible journey we are on. Many do. And chances of that gift reappearing are slim. Sometimes we could close down an addictive mode of the "poor me's" and grab on to old habits. We find too many excuses. We are triggered by fear and self-doubt.

If we are brave enough to slay the ego once, we can do it again and again. But the first session where we show up to one of our dragons is the most important. When we finally move out of fear in a little decision, our big decisions will follow.

Then there is a euphoric thrill in the looking…the searching for the one thing that tells us what our next right purpose is and how to move into it. It comes through and we are free. We finally listened. It's a great story. It's our story and we hear it.

When self-doubt sets in the next time we slay, move on and we are victorious again. The key here is the gift of the word "again." If we are still having trouble figuring out if this will work for us, we can look at the following thought:

Are we one of the talented souls that are up for the journey or are we one of those souls that suffer from the journey? Where are we in this moment, in this stage of our life? Do we think about all the "if's?" And, are we allowing the "should's" to take over. Are they the main contenders representing our overactive egos?

If we are really ready to silence the ego, we must move head-on to a final destination if we ever hope to reach our state of *NIRVANA. Every Spiritual Leader and Sage throughout the ages assures us that we may have peace. Granted there are some who tell us that we have to wait until we get a first class ticket to Heaven. But new thoughts that are surfacing are telling us that our Heaven can be right here in the here and now.* There will be no need for "what if's" or "should's." It is just.

Some may believe that Nirvana is a single state of being. And if that works for these souls, it's okay. It well may be the stepping stone to realizing that it is more than that. Nirvana encompasses all that there is into one level of peaceful existence. It can and does live everywhere that we are if we access it with the tools that we are given through listening to our hearts. Being impeccable with our word, never assuming anything, not taking anything personally and always doing our best is a book by Don Miguel Ruiz called "THE FOUR AGREEMENTS". By accomplishing The Four Agreements, we are destined to a life of enlightenment and peace.

Deletion of negative responses about our life or the life of others, changes our history. Our egos that are not our friend fade away, because that is where negativity is born and does live. Our new journey becomes one of sight-seeing and showing up by participation. Life is no longer a dreaded day of just marching through to our final in destination. Our journeys are softer, easier, and more comfortable. And why is this? Because we recognize that we are being guided and loved. We are done questioning what we know is true.

It is a time when we intuitively are not alone. We are usually not sure why we feel so guided and loved but we do. There are all indications that our life is on track and that we are on track.

We will be championed by our angels, guides, and loved ones. The cheering section will be everywhere we go. It is obvious and we will be welcomed into a peaceful enlightened nurtured self-reality with open arms.

OUR LIFE CAN BE HARD...OR NOT! REALLY!

So with all the changes that we can feel coming our way at various enlightened points in our life, there is just one more choice. Shall I decide to make this hard or is there another way? Really? Really, there is another way. But that other way sometimes feels hard. The question to pose to oneself may be, "Would it be harder not to try something different or harder to stay in the rut we are already in?" No one...no one but us gets to make that decision. We make or we don't. We may make it today or a year from now or never. Still, this is our choice. The judgment that we may have been raised with is not judging us but we are sure to be doing a good job of judging ourselves if we do not make a positive change.

The seekers get their treasures in the form of Spiritual Riches. The stay-at-home *non-seekers* will choose to stay at home, and suffer with Emotional Rags. The Universe is always waiting for us to choose a life of purpose. That is why we get to experience our Emotional Rags that lead us to an opportunity of Spiritual awakening. And then the Riches of life so abundantly appear. We just cannot stop them.

When we identify the Emotional Rags to uncover the Riches, we are more than halfway there. So how hard do we want this to be? It can be very hard work, or it can be something we just start showing up to. Showing up is going to work if we do things differently. It even may be a good idea to take a different way to work, go to a different grocery store, and travel to places that we go to frequently by going another route. We need to change one thing...and we will find out that the change is everything.

THE SECRET SAUCE IS SLOWING DOWN

My mother made the best Italian sauce for our spaghetti dinners. It took three days on low heat and then it had to set still. In the quiet of our kitchen, it would absorb all the life of the meats, the tomatoes, the garlic, the onion, and whatever else my mother magically added. One ingredient was to only share with me. The secret was in the sauce. We too, need to take our time, one day at a time and add all the ingredients that will make us better equipped to have a tasty life. We too, need to slow down and simmer so that we can absorb our new way of thinking. So there is a secret but it is not well kept anymore. The cat is out of the bag. Slowing down and feeling the texture in our lives, listening to the percolation, and then doing a taste test to see how we are doing is a recipe for anyone including addictive compulsive people. Instead of living like "Instant Oatmeal" we are finding a better way. Fast living is also fast dying. We either leave the earth ahead of schedule or we leave not seeing, feeling, or knowing any one including ourselves.

So there are no secrets to having it all. Granted, we cannot have everything, but we can have it all - that is - all that we choose to have. If we are in our right mind, we will be living our affirmations. We will affirm the good and leave the rest to God.

TAKING A SLOW BOAT TO CHINA, OR LOST?

An old saying like "stuck at sea" or "lost at sea" can be our stuck point for the "'wanna' be" sailors. Being a sailor and wanting to be one are two very different mindsets. If we sit on shore and look out over the water to see the beauty of the wind grabbing a sailboat's sail is much different from sailing the vessel. What would it take to be your own sailor? When do we stop talking about who we are, what we are and what we want to be and start showing up to all that chattering ego spilling out into conversations as if we were the star we pretend to be. Do we need a nudge to get going? Sometimes we just do. So what, if we need a nudge then we start asking for one. Find the support in your friends and family that will fulfill your dreams by encouraging you to just do it.

The universe has a very interesting way of getting our attention. Do you ever remember being stopped in a certain direction, or being stopped because you were not thinking straight and were making bad decisions or worse yet no decisions at all?

Some of us are more fortunate, and have not experienced the deep despair of Emotional Rags that are born from addiction, suicide, and/or suicidal thoughts. Others have to go through passive aggressive relationships, and/or thoughtless and selfish lives. If that's what it takes, many have said that's what it takes.

Maybe we do need to over-eat or have poor intimate relationships. Something has to get our attention. But is this just the tip of the iceberg? Why do we do such destructive behaviors? Are we doing everything to escape even the possibility of healing. It seems so.

Our emotional iceberg is sitting well above the water line with the rest plunged deep into the sea of our distress. Spotting our iceberg is good but we need to realize that spotting the iceberg is just the beginning of melting the rest of our poor thinking habits away. We can melt away distrust, disease resentments, judgments and a host of other egoic opinions that we brought to our life for years.

So in this state of discovery, who has been judging us? Is it a wrathful God or is it ourselves? Being stopped dead in our tracks does not mean we are being judged but it does mean we are being loved. We are loved enough to have an opportunity of changing our outdated thinking. We are having a chance to be a "Rags to Riches" story and now we will have the chance to feel the love we have and always have had.

SELF-JUDGMENT THAT EATS AWAY OUR SANITY

"I am my our own worst enemy!" How many times have we heard ourselves or someone else say that?

The only judgment from a loving Universe comes from those who judge themselves or from we who find ourselves in a rhythm of self-analogy of everything we can find wrong about ourselves. If we are doing just that, we will not feel as if we are on time or living in a perfect universe where our lives unfold perfectly.

When we are living in addictive behaviors there is no room for sanity. We are not thinking clearly and have no desire to do anything but feed our addiction. We may well know that we have a problem but our self-justification totally gives us permission to continue doing what we are doing. Most addictive people are very hard on themselves. Whether it is their work, their drinking or drugging, it hardly matters as self- judgment gives them a reason to keep doing what they are doing. For these people, there is no time to consider stopping. The sanity they could acquire by coming clean about who they really are is not something that they find desirable. They would rather live victimized and give their addictions top billing for their uncontrollable lives.

Even though we live in a universe that travels in perfect synchronization, we are not going to feel that order and its gifts when we are in active addiction. A universe of love and light will elude us. Our souls are not in sync with a God of our understanding or a universe that offers messages and information for all that we may need. Over the centuries the word "God" has been so misused, especially in regards to wrathful punishment for all that we are not, as to being in God's favor, that many are no longer able to digest a loving God that may be helpful. It may help to call this Higher Conscious State a "Higher Power," "The Earth," "The Universe." Coming to grips with allowing revenge and punishment is a good start in healing self-inflicted wounds of a life that has kept us locked in any kind of despair caused by any kind of situation.

Even biblically, after all the blood and guts of the Old Testament, we are shown a Christ, with a Christ-consciousness who is telling us to love our neighbor, to help our neighbor, and to be open to all those who need our help. His life and example are well-documented as one that brought the teachings of love to a time in history that, up until that point, was extremely judgmental. The earth was receiving a new message. A message that was welcomed and one that still has not taken over globally. Yet it still had a positive impact on the future of humanity. We documented records of the Buddha giving the same message, one of enlightenment and hope; a message of self-love and kindness.

So the obvious is that judgment is our way of holding ourselves back from being and having more.

If we want to get rid of our enemy, we can do so quickly. We are it! And when we have slayed our own dragon, we will become prodigal to our Source and Supply and come home to whom we really are. Without self-judgment we dump our Rags and embrace our Riches.

COMPARING IS SELF-JUDGMENT DISGUISED

There will be times, in our human experience, when our observing turns into comparing with others, and self-judgment. We may feel we are ahead of others or worse yet, we do not measure up. What we do not realize when we are comparing or self-judging is that we have assumed that we really know another soul's life story.

However we try to compare or judge ourselves is one thing but to judge and compare ourselves with someone else cannot work. In order to understand another soul, we would have to be living and walking in their footsteps. This is impossible. It is a total waste of time and takes our focus away from ourselves and the next right thing to do.

Assumption is always dangerous territory because it has no life except the life we give it. With assumption, we leave our own journey to observe and compare another's to ourselves only to be disappointed; to find out that they are empty and not available to our own journey.

There is a loss of time and we are unable to hear or listen to the still small voice that lives within us. We are too busy chattering about what we do or do not assume about another person. Our journeys are left floundering. Thinking that another has it better, we do not know how well we already have what we have. Our lives are playing out as they should. Others' lives are playing out as they should. Once we embrace the similarities and value the differences we come to a time of accelerated growth.

Why not take the journey we are in and learn to think differently? When we change our thinking we change our lives. In this moment of self-clarity we find ourselves committed to our own journey and being the champion to all others. If we really want to feel good, we will learn the way of the Spiritual Warrior who is a champion to self and thus to others.

The gifting of praise and recognition to another is a very successful way to live.

Thinking of others creates a body full of energy starting from the heart as it opens up and we become willing to share our journey in the attempt to help another and become one.

There will be times we are struggling. And for those times, just by standing in the wings of life, we can feel our good energy and still send it out. That is, if we are willing to abort and release our self-absorbed, addictive nature to another dimension.

Sending out affirmative messages heals the messenger as well as the one being sent such a positive energized thought of recognition. What are we recognizing? Does it matter? Recognizing another soul's positive journey is the key to living our lives addiction free.

The energy sent from our hearts verbally or silently is powerful. It will radiate the message of compassion, healing, oneness, and love.

Judgments cannot exist in this environment. They cease to exist. When we are living with addictions we do not have this kind of positive purpose. But once free of selfish hiding and using our addiction, co-creation with others sets in. Do we mean to be this way? Most of the time we are unaware and these are the times we are guided and loved through a situation that we are not capable of maneuvering at that particular moment.

We are becoming co-creators with everything that we touch. Little by little with the loss of our addictive nature we can know exactly what to do. We are here on the planet with a purpose and we become very obvious.

Oneness in daily life is recognizable. We see each other in a different light. We recognize the evolution of the journey of others and we are a part of them without being them.

This is yet again another of the biggest Spiritual Riches in this life time that we could ever acquire. By eliminating comparisons and learning how to co-create with others puts us in a new class room full of information. We have arrived...again.

Souls attract the light that allows total clarity. But as all Spiritual Gifts, we are asked to walk the winding road so we need to understand what it takes. When we get there, we will be able to SEE. Really SEE. Answers are revealed.

If we have been experiencing a restless state, we will find our spirit comes into a state of calmness and Nirvana. Some may scoff at such a statement. They do not understand...yet. That is understandable and no judgment is needed on souls that have not yet received more information. It takes readiness, spiritual awareness, and trust in process to be able to have this gift.

Are we back to willingness to change our narrow outdated thinking? Yes.

ONENESS VS SEPARATION

ONENESS is and always has been our connection to everything. But for many of us we have never recognized how connected to everything we are. A chattering ego has kept us busy with the past and the future.

Why do we go through periods of feeling very separate or even abandoned? For everyone it is different and yet the same. Feeling separate or abandoned from our tribe is an inside job that needs to be attended to.

If there is a feeling of separation, it is most likely because we have slipped into seclusion.

We may feel that we do not measure up to others. And if we feel that way, others will sense this feeling, too. It is not easy to hide negative energy and if we do it takes a great deal of effort. And if our wounded separation in the form of seclusion is noticed by others, it will often create even more separation for both parties.

To heal and leave this state of self-destruction, our thinking has to change. The focus on what we are not will have to go so that we can start taking stock of what we really are. There is not a soul on the planet that is not here to share special gifts. By letting go and letting God show through our persona's self-destructive nature, there will be no room to live in a healthy, exposed soul.

Others have their gifts to share with us, too. In a oneness principle, recognizing that we are all here breathing the same air and sharing the planet leaves no room or need for any kind of self-judgment. Without self-judgment, judging others comes to be a very hard thing to do. Separation is an emotional rag that holds us hostage until we release it. We will have help. Willingness again is the key. Once willing, any rag we want to heal is already healing.

Self-esteem is not egotistical. Rather it is a healthy knowledge of our good. When we have healthy self-esteem, Emotional Rags are non-existent.

Leaving the souls that are struggling with their own self-worth is not abandonment. The time will come to listen to the winds of change in their own lives. Being there at that time is the greatest gift to those who are in the process of healing their Emotional Rags. This is when they really need us. We become available to help them through our loving, open, and affirming commitment to their healing. We share our story to help them know they are not alone and are on track.

When it is time to be connected to those who are healing, the right person always shows up just as it does for all of us.

We will sense our deep compassion for others. Everyone is gifted at that moment in time. This is yet another lesson in humility as we let go of our old ways of living and thinking. We are finally here for the grand finale of our lives when it comes to treating our fellow travelers with compassion and understanding without a need to even comment.

It would be good to conclude that we are not here to live and work in separation. It is not only lonely, but unproductive in the ability to receive the joint gifts of the Universe; the gifts of mind, body, and spirit. Success in this life cannot come to us without the loving gifts of others. We cannot live successfully without the gifts of others.

CALL GOD WHAT YOU LIKE...IT'S ALL GOOD!

We were born of God and God lives within everything. For most of us that is not hard to understand. However, there are those who have difficulty with even the word God. Understandably so and why wouldn't some have a problem with a threatening, judgmental god. A god of childhood that will have us cower in fear. A god that tells us that we can never be good enough?

Which century started all of that damaging thought to a loving presence of Spirit and why? Historically, there are definite times where power was more important than a loving god. Don't you muse how God thought about all that punishment surrounded by fear so that a few more shillings would drop into the collection plate? Or a few more taxes could be taken by the church and the Kings and their Kingdoms so that parishioners were driven out of fear to their weekly pews where they were asked to give even more. It was their money that bought their heaven or so the story from the pulpit blasted out to the people.

When money came to the church in the form of greed, greed became the God of fear.

These were fearful times when Kings and Kingdoms along with the church used fear of Hell and fire to control.

This was a violent and sad time in history that has been well documented. Unfortunately, there still is fear that has some of the residuals of a doctrine that is still used for control.

When a human beings live in fear, they have a flight mechanism that kicks in. And one of those flights will take a fearful person right to any addiction that will take them out of their fear. Times are changing because the young people of today are not buying this fear. But there are still many souls that struggle with the Rags of fear and use their addictive life to escape the ravaging threats that do not even exist. Fear in its purest form is a total loss of freedom. This is something that needs to be revealed to anyone suffering from fear. Everyone has the chance to let it go. Everyone will get the chance. Not everyone will be ready but just knowing that there is something bigger than ourselves can release these illusions is a billboard of hope that will not go unnoticed. The Emotional Rags of addiction have a time and place to heal. There are certain experiences that have to take place before the addictive one is ready to jump ship and head for the land of opportunity.

Many of us were told as children of God that fear was necessary to have God's approval. There were consequences if we did not obey the rules of the written word. And for a truthful human being, there would be no way to keep the rules that were set before us. We were not here to be perfect but to learn. The learning lessons through living out our lessons were a forgotten and ignored teaching in our schools and churches. So why wouldn't tormented, not-good-enough souls seek an addiction to take them out of that false, inaccessible world?

This kind of mindset only births a good dose of Emotional Rags. Why even Old Saint Nick has gotten a bad rap. He lives at the North Pole, he watches us like a god and as children we have to be good for approximately 30 days or we have been warned there will be no presents under the Christmas Tree. Why would we want to leave cookies and hot chocolate at midnight for a guy who has been spying on us all year? With this kind of message to children, adults, too, have a message that they will be caught doing something bad, having a bad thought, not getting what they want. So instead of Santa being a myth, he may still live in the minds of many as they go through their lives holding onto the fears of no presents, going to Hell, and that the pearly gates have a pad lock on them. And St. Peter is playing cards on some cloud and ignoring the pleas for entry to the Heavenly Realms of perfection.

Why would anyone want to wait for Heaven when the Heaven they want is one that they provide in this life? It takes the waiting game out of play. Our misery on earth changes to our joy and extravagant magnificence just being here. Yes, we are going to make some mistakes. Yes, we will or will not learn from them. But in the end we will be loved for all that we have tried to do to show up to our lives and the lives of others. The monster of a God does not live in the bog of our consciousness unless we put God there. The loving God can be a dragon, a thought, a moment of realization that comes through our hearts. We are connected. We will know God the minute we want to have this incredible relationship.

There were too many times that parents and peers misguided us because of their own deep-rooted fears. They were taught fear and never healed that fear from their parents. When does the story of fear stop? We stop it. We are the ones.

Times had to change. Misguided false information has taken a toll on religion. It had to happen.

Maybe we have finally gone back to the truth of this thing called life. For a God that was always here and always will be, we too are a part of the always. But have we been misled to think that there are rules to be loved? Turning within to our spirituality, which is the truth that lives within, will give us all the answers and connection to a God that is not going anywhere but is right with us the moment we access this power. Those who are using God have not accessed the power. They think they are the power. For those of us who have had the gift of messages through our quiet meditative times with the God of our understanding, know that there are some who have not found their way. There are some deeply wounded souls that are filled with darkness and are so dark they are illuminating the light that is so bright. There is so much of it that it will do what it does. It will overtake the darkness.

Where does our loving God sit with these dark souls? Some are addicted to killing, booze, gambling, bullying. Their Emotional Rags still have a speck of light that can at any point come through. In which lifetime will that happen? It will happen when it should. Our job is to carry the lighted torch that shines in all corners, on all planets, in the face of every star. We do that simply by being light and learning how to overcome addictive behaviors so that we can be of service to the truth of this beautiful Universe.

Spirituality is the connection of having a God within to communicate what has always been. Call it what you like, but there is a Higher Power for all of us. Any soul may have it. We are the curtain calls to truth every time we overcome hate, fear, or any other discomfort that takes us away from our heartfelt messages. Addiction takes us away. It can cause us to be dark. But the light is there and the second we start to heal addictive behavior we feel the sand bags lifted off our shoulders. We are free again to walk the earth and be in an experience of discovery instead of being discovered for all we are not.

Spirituality is center stage in today's world. It is coming through the souls who have been incarnated in this generation. With today's enlightened information, there is a new breeze blowing and it can be felt in all the houses of religion and in spiritual centers. It can be felt in small groups, schools, acceptance of life-styles, and letting discrimination take a hike so that we all can see the world as being color- blind when it comes to souls.

Those who have lived with a vengeful God and are looking to a Higher Power that falls under a more loving category, which relates to love and compassion, will be pleasantly surprised when they start waking up to today.

Understanding that there is something greater than oneself does not seem to be a hard sell for most. By taking a breath and letting all our questions go streaming into a Universe that is alive and well... will give us answers. It may take a few tries but it does work.

Analyzing God, the Universe and ourselves... becomes of little importance when we are brought to a quiet realization of why we are here.

We will be told. It will come to us. We may not be listening but without addictive behavior there will be a time when we hear the news release as to what we are here to do. Many of us are well-engaged in our Spiritual Contract. We may realize that there is more than one. Why not? Who wants to be bored when the contracts become too easy or are finished? Even that paper route or selling ice cream at the carnival could have well been a contract. Think what happened with your smaller contracts. Who did you meet? What did you learn? Where did it take you?

We are here to live and learn so much. Maybe our purpose for a while needs to be the lesson of addiction. Oh, well. It may be the only thing that catches our attention for wanting to change. We all get wake up calls.

Once shedding our own addictions and coming to our knees to say, "Hey, Thanks," we will find ourselves quite different around those who are caught in the addictive life style. It becomes less complicated to look at others and judge their addictions.

Compassion is another gift that comes from our experiences with Emotional Rags related to addiction. The heartache of addiction and what it takes to heal becomes a compassionate road of showing up to help others. We know the pain. We know the freedom. We are there to share that addiction which is only the tip of the iceberg of why and for what reason we chose to escape into a world that would only hide us for just so long.

Addiction has a purpose and the main purpose is to give us a purpose. By giving up judgment with others, we compassionately apply it to all addictive behaviors of others. So here we are showing up to our life's purpose for the time we need to give away love and information to another so they can have what we do: Peace.

More is always revealed. Being alive means that the stream of on-going information keeps coming as long as we are open to it.

We will experience several awakenings in a life time. What we do with the awakenings is what will manifest in this life-time. What others do is none of our business. What we do is our business.

The Emotional Rags of our past leave us with the Riches of our present which do become known. We are the builders of hope and trust, and we dump fear for freedom. Futures are no longer planned in detail as we begin to know that living in the present moment is building our future. Every day is a building block and we design the architecture of our lives with skill because our foundation is eternally and solidly connected. We are the future of our intention in every now moment we embrace. With this kind of a change in thinking we are not missing a beat in our lives. We have learned to SEE. Why would we not want to change out addiction to a life of SEEING? That is another one of the biggest Spiritual Riches we will receive. How could we turn it down? Some will. Some are not ready. But when the lesson is over and the soul is ready, all of this and more will be patiently waiting for their discovery.

So, to overstimulate, over-theorize, or over intellectualize something that just is? Life is a gift that unfolds and answers are revealed at the most appropriate time. By living in the moment we will know all that there is to know. This is what builds our future.

GUIDES, ANGELS AND LOVED ONES ARE HERE

Some may say that to believe in the energy of others who have gone on is scary, not true, or just plain ridiculous. For some this could feel to be their truth. But if the chattering ego has totally absorbed their minds and they have not been able to hear anything but a party line of voices instructing and jabbering fear of possibilities that steal their freedom, they will not feel the presence of the energy of continuing life that surrounds them. They will not be able to allow in the guides that have been with them since birth.

The loved ones will be unable to chime in until the chatter settles down and we can actually hear and feel the love that has always been with us and is constantly circling our every moment.

Those of us who have learned the gift of meditation, quieting down and asking for help, have the stories to share of how they are being guided. Dreams, out of the blue help, and messages presented from strangers are just some of the many ways we are saved from ourselves. There seems to always come a time in our lives when we remember a miracle that saved us from a challenging situation. These wake-up moments are learning times where we are being reminded that there is something that is unexplainable guiding us during certain times in our earthly lives. Learning to become centered and quiet will give us the gift of knowing many things that we may have thought that we never had access to before.

Usually when we are least expecting a helping hand, anything can happen. Those "out of the blue" moments can also be a stranger giving us unexpected help or the message we need to move on. These messages of help can come to us in many ways that are just not explainable. At the time we really don't care how we get the help. We are too grateful to analyze how or why it happened.

Many times in active addiction, there is help from the other side. There is a layer of protection over us that keeps us and others safe for as long as possible. Can it be proven? Can it not be proven? Ask a recovered person if they have ever recognized in their sobriety that they were saved from themselves many times before they finally sobered up. It may be hard to understand what is helping us along our way but the truth is we are always being protected, guided, watched and loved. This is true in addiction or out of addiction. There is no one left out of the love of the Universe. The only way to be left out is to fail to realize it for ourselves. Chatter will keep this message away from us. As we learn to quiet the mind, the chatter loses power and the real power can be felt circling around us.

Believing it or not does not stop these miracles from happening. But not recognizing the powers that are available for us alters our right action to receive the best of the gifts that are trying to be presented.

If we find ourselves struggling with doubt, or fear and cannot seem to embrace that we are being loved from the other side, so be it. We may not be ready to fully surrender to the oneness that exists in our Universe. We are not being forced to believe. There is no race and no time table to access these gifts. However, if by chance we find ourselves staying open to all possibilities, we will someday find ourselves feeling the help that has been with us all along. No one is forcing us to listen to our hearts instead of our head. But what a very kind thing to do for ourselves. Does not the kindness to others start with how we respect and treat ourselves?

As a friendly Universe of Spiritual Riches patiently awaits us, waiting to gift us to our right of Riches, it is comforting to know that we are not being judged for the time it takes to get us where we need to be. Yet time in a timeless Universe, is our right to passage when we are ready.

The question arises, can we learn all we need to learn in one life-time? If we are timeless and have a deep knowing that we are moving on, could it be that it takes longer to master all that we need to know? Will we be given the time and is this what the sages of old, including the Christ and the Buddha mean about enlightenment? To ascend to a Higher Self, does not a soul need the entire experience of multiple journeys to find the Christ within? These are only questions that we ourselves can ponder and come to a knowing of what we are ready to take on. Our Guides, and our Angels and our Loved Ones can be messengers to help us with these questions. The closer we get to a transition from this life to the next is usually when many of us open up to the possibilities of what is ahead for us. Do we have to wait for our Riches? Are our lives only the Rags of getting through or getting by? Or are the Riches in our now the second we know that they are available? The answer lives within. It becomes a time of clarity void of separation.

PERSONAL JOURNEYS ARE WHAT WE ARE

Our personal journey is what we are doing now. We are all on one even if it feels like we are not. It could feel like the wrong one but it is what we are doing right now. It will stay the same until the journey changes or we change or both. We are alive and being alive means we are on our journey until journey's end.

If done well, or not done well, we are still in our life's journey and it is affecting everything that we are doing along with any family or friends or strangers with whom we engage. We cannot help but have an effect on everyone with whom we come into contact. And so it is true for those who touch our lives. We are all in this together and our journeys either become non-reactive or reactive to everything that confronts us. We will always have a choice as to how we want to experience our life. Will we react or will we be non-reactive in the sense that we take none of our experiences personally? If we choose not to be offended with life and its daily experiences, we will be blessed with constant new ways of thinking which will offer us multiple choices. We will start over as many times as we need to. Fear will not take our freedom. And freedom will give us the bridge from our Emotional Rags to our Spiritual Riches.

We will find that we are lessons for some and healing for others. We will not be left out of this equation as we will find that our lessons will be in front of us as well. They will stay with us until we heal. We all get a turn. There is no one left out and if we know this it becomes easier to love our way through our changes.

Could it be that lessons are like a class we attend for things we want to know? Is a class with lessons the way we learn to be the shining light we are here to be? By not reacting to our lessons, we are a much quicker study of our own healing process. But if reacting is our lesson, then let's do it and get it over with. It will have its consequences but we must need it if we keep doing it. Staying stuck in a lesson is a grueling way to live for any length of time but if that is our path out of reacting and learning our lessons, then that is exactly the lesson we will be attracting. Being a quick learner is very rewarding but learning what we need to learn under all circumstances is what we are here to do.

Being available to a formula of change will present our Spiritual gifts more quickly. The formula is not complex. It lives in our now moments. Our job with our life is to just show up.

So one may ask, how do we know what the formula is or is not? And what does it look like?

When life is working, we always know the feeling of freedom and fearless living. If our life is not working, then the fear, depression, anxiety and doubt is circling us like a wolf on a rabbit. Heading in the right direction, we are soaring with the wind and not against it. Life flows. It is a time of ease.

However, if our way of life is not moving in a smooth direction and we are determined to make it go a certain way, and we are pushing it to do so, we have created a storm that can pass with little intensity or become an F5 tornado taking everything we touch in our path.

The easiest way to weave into the eye of a storm so that we can find some peace and quiet time to assimilate answers from our Higher Conscious Self is a simple request to the God of our understanding. Ask for help. Ask for guidance. It will come. It has to. It has been promised. Surrendering and listening will put us on course with good orderly direction (G.O.D.). We need the lesson of "letting go and letting God" for as many times as it takes to learn that letting go is our only salvation...for anything.

The God that we go to is our personal God, our Senior Partner, our confidant. We may call this Higher Energy anything we want if the word God seems to get in the way of a prayer or a question. The Universe knows who you are talking to if the heart is involved.

By healing our own Emotional Rags, learning to listen and surrender, we become a healing mechanism to others. Maybe this is our first reason for being here. Our own Rags heal more quickly once we share compassion and empathy with those who are still struggling with their own Emotional Rags. It is easier to understand another when we too understand what it feels like to be lost in Emotional Rags and to feel as if there is no way out.

How fortunate that we can gain the insight to our own lives when we are able to understand, love, and be a source of compassion for others under all circumstances. Because circumstances are always circumstances and very personally felt. Does it really matter what the circumstance is when it comes to helping another? We will find we have much more to give as we participate in recognizing the oneness in others.

WALKING OUR TALK...WHAT A CONCEPT!
We say we are walking our talk. What are we talking about? Are we just spouting off what others should do? Are we doing what we need to do ourselves to reach a higher conscious state? Or are we in the business of making others feel small and making ourselves feel greater than?

It is very hard to be free when we are trapped with what we feel others should be doing. However, there is not much need to talk when our walk is really telling our story. It can be very freeing to be present to our own everyday living. What we are thinking, what we are doing, and how we are doing it is the walk that needs not long explanation. If there comes a time when others are curious and ask questions as to why our lives seem to be doing so well...that is the time to share our own story. This is not the time to tell others what they should do.

If we are to take a good hard, fearless look at our walk, we can observe if it really is married to our talk. Silent pictures had a lot to say in the 1920's and the audience had a lot of time to watch the drama without the drama of sound. Does this mean we are not to engage in conversation or does this mean that we need to first listen and then engage with a sense of sharing our stories and how we walked through our self-talk to get where we needed to go.

Addiction comes in many forms. It can switch its face from food to drink, to sex, to gambling, to lies, to drugs. Only we can assess our own walk to find out if it has been on track.

So has our walk been on track or has there been a need to escape our world and its changes and challenges with addictive behaviors? Telling others what to do or not do could lead us into a new or an old addiction. We will need the great escape. We have not been coming from our hearts but coming from our heads and now we are in another emotional rag that needs healing...the ego. We will need something to make us feel better. We will be looking and hoping that we will be taken out of our self-justification that we know it all. Many are in this misery without even knowing why they are feeling the way they do.

Without being truthful, transparent and authentic we have become finger-pointers and we have four of our own pointing right back at ourselves. That just does not and cannot feel good.

The great escape is back to addiction. Any addiction that comes in any way we think, will make us feel good in the moment.

Addictive people in or out of addiction are masters at finding ways to feel good temporarily. They never think at the time it will be temporary until they come out of this state of the "quick fix". We want to feel better fast. Our willingness becomes an action step into self-destruct instead of self-healing. We do feel better temporarily. However, if we have let the drugs and alcohol go, we may still be finding ways such as eating, sleeping, sex, or gambling, just a few of the behaviors we will adopt so that we do not have to face ourselves. We can pretend that we are just fine the way we are and that our know-it-all attitude with others was well intended and deserved.

The Universe does have a sense of humor. Did we really think we were getting away with anything? When we wake up hung over and sick we are back in the reality of who we are and it is ten times worse than it was before we checked how to forget what we did.

For the people who are in recovery and no longer using drugs for the great escape, it is easy to unintentionally fall into something else that will take them out of their pain and give them a temporary feel-good moment. In both cases it does not last. The difference being that the person in recovery has people to call, meetings to go to, and friends and sponsors to help change their life to one that is more authentic and honest and has no need of any addictive substance or cop-out of any kind.

When we are finally ready to gift ourselves a total change in thinking, our fellow travelers, will be there to help us to step to the beat of a different drummer. Becoming a different drummer is the way we give ourselves the self-identity to be present to the world we live in. We become available to be of value without the need to sidestep our responsibilities or to check up for a temporary feel good moment.

One of the tools of sidestepping any kind of slip leading us back to our old life and old way of thinking is to not remember what it was really like. But if we are slipping, we cannot help remembering as we are right back where we were only this time it is even worse.

Addiction brings us to our knees. That is its job. Many have lost almost everything, harmed their friends and family, lost jobs, homes, and cars. So if we have slipped we need to do whatever it takes to once again come to our senses. Picking up where we left off is a winning solution. We live in a Universe that will guide us. There are plenty of souls that will and do show up exactly at the right time. There will be chance meetings and out of the blue situations that seem to be coincidences, but are not. We all live on time even when we are out of step. There will be those who will show up to love us until we can love ourselves. Our job is to recognize them when they arrive.

The wake-up call for anyone with an addiction is always a hard one. But was there any other way? Something had to get our attention. When the quick fix of addiction no longer works life wants us back. Trying to run back to our addiction no longer works. We are being called to our Higher Self. When the jig is up...there just is no other way, short of death to give us another chance at who we really are in this life. Addiction requires a hard wake up call. It just does.

It has always been a proven fact that addictive people are especially bad at listening. They are always planning their next round of self-indulgence. The only thing they are listening to is how to get there. Life revolves around addiction not the art of being good listeners. We have always been in control and now we are finding that the only time we can be in control of our lives, is to be totally out of control. We need the connection that gives us the intuitive counseling that we need to follow. Without having the help from a Higher Source, staying clean can be little more than a very sad and dry experience. Without guidance from a Higher Source and people who are going to love us until we can finally love ourselves, there is little hope of success. That is why recovery programs are so valuable. Everyone that is in recovery knows how each other feels. Sharing those feelings keeps us clean for one day at a time. Slipping and sliding around an addiction is insane. Just ask someone who has gone back to that way of life. Even the hiders eventually cannot hide anymore.

Interestingly, others were well aware of what we were doing to ourselves as hard as it was to hide it. Here is a personal story that I would like to share.

I was one of "those guys that drank like a sailor," and did it every day. When I tried to sober up and could not I thought I was fooling the people around me. How would anyone know as long as I acted like my normal self whom even I had not seen for years. I was sure after a few months of sobriety that my diagnosis of being an alcoholic must surely be wrong. I was also sure that I no longer needed to work on my so called addiction which I decided was a terrible mistake.

So what if I had a family of heavy drinkers and alcoholics on both my mother's side and father's side of the family. That was their problem, not mine. I just got too stressed. At this welcome point of discovery I saw an opening that had a drink in it. I thought that I needed that drink and I was sure I could drink responsibly.

So after I decided that I could drink again, I found myself monitoring my drinking. I would only have two glasses of wine instead of the vineyard quantity I used to consume.

It did not take long for me to end up as a daily drinker. I had made a covenant with the God of my understanding that if I had a problem again that I would return to the program of Alcoholic Anonymous. By the time

I did, I had quit a job, my back had gone out, and I needed to be rescued by my best friend's family. They came again and scraped me off the floor and got me back to a small town where they lived so that I could recover from what they wanted to believe was an on- going back problem that I had had for quite a few years.

But there was more to my story as I had mixed alcohol and pain killers to fix my back that had gone out and I ended up being a total mess. I was unable to think or function as the drugs and alcohol together could have easily killed me. But my Higher Power was not done with me yet and I lived, and suffered through many months of trying to think straight and get back in AA. I was unable to sober up. I prayed, I begged the God of my understanding to let me be sober again, but I could not stay sober.

The part of this story I find amusing today is remembering my little morning drinking routine. I would be drinking in the morning and of course doing my best to hide it. So, instead of a cup of coffee, I would have a cup of red wine. Yes, it was in my coffee cup. I was sure no one would guess that I was having my first of many drinks of the day. But did they guess? Did they know what I was doing? Of course they did. How can anyone with purple lips and a purple tongue early in the morning be drinking coffee? Today I share this experience because my addiction would not leave me alone. It would not let up. I needed help from something much greater than myself. I had asked for help before and gotten it. This time I had to fight to be heard. My sincerity was in play and I was only going to get Supreme help if I was really ready to commit. I was.

I was called back to work. That was my first miracle. I showed up, but as soon as I got off the plane, I went right to the bar and ordered a glass of wine. This time, however, I could not drink it. I was not able to get it down. This was a total surprise. It tasted terrible and I got sick to my stomach on the first sip. I left a full glass of wine which was not something that was normal for me to do.

Two days later, I showed up to an AA meeting and the next sponsor I would have for the next few years, was a man that was 25 years sober. He saw the desperation in my eyes. I told him that I had slipped back into the disease of alcoholism and that I was so ashamed for being so stupid as I had not been able to sober up. I let him know that I had some significant time in the AA program before I headed out on my own to prove that I was not an alcoholic. My new sponsor, with a smile on his face reached out to me and with a look of total sincerity said quietly and calmly, "Just pick up where you left off and you will be fine." Go to a meeting every day, get a sponsor, and work the Twelve steps of Alcoholics Anonymous.

This stranger that I had just met, spent the rest of the day with me. We talked, I listened. I was finally at peace. He became my sponsor and as the years rolled by, I called him every year to thank him for that very special liberating day.

That was 16 years ago. I know today that the God of my understanding had a plan all worked out and as I showed up, the plan showed up to me. The obsession was finally lifted years ago. It has never returned. I can go to restaurants, bars, down isles in grocery stores that have legal beverages that could kill me and I have no desire to have a drink under any circumstances. I am among many that have been blessed.

Addiction for me was alcohol. But addiction comes in many disguises. We can be addicted to people, places and things. We can have a drug and alcohol problem that we can conquer over time to find ourselves buried in another addiction. Everyone has help with an emotional rag to get to their Spiritual Riches. For whatever reason something in our life goes wrong. If we take a deep breath before reacting, we will find that the answers for what is happening to us will unfold with clarity and sensibility.

IT TAKES WHAT IT TAKES

Do we listen to advice from others? Are we willing to give up our own way to let a new and better way unfold? What does it take for the Universe to get our attention? It takes what it takes.

Can we, addictive persons, be guided and fixed? The answer is 99.9% no. Is there someone else who has the magic cure to fix anyone with an addiction?

When someone else gives the old college try, it just gives the addictive person more time to be addictive. This fixing of any addiction is an inside job. The inside job begins when the Emotional Rags have hit an all-time low. At this low point a decision out of desperation can be made. There is a time when enough is enough. The jig is up and the fat lady finally sings.

A glimpse of hope or desperation may be filtering through the foggy thinking. It can peek through even with all that pain. We know that we finally have to find a way of living that is free of addiction.

Do we always listen? Only when we are hurting so badly that we have nowhere else to go.

In some miraculous way we are listening to that still small voice that is the God of our understanding. That voice is reaching out to us and offering us a way out of our Rags. We do not know the way yet, but we feel there may be one. In most cases, for most people it seems hopeful but impossible.

Why does it take some of us to hit such a hard rock bottom? When asking people why they waited so long to come out of the darkness into the light of their lives, most could not answer why it took so long and life had to become so hard.

It just takes what it takes. It always has for anyone coming out of the throes of addiction. Could it be that part of our time on earth is to finally get the lessons we need to get? The unhealthy ego holds us tightly to the ropes not letting us escape. But when we do, we find the compassion and understanding to be present for others.

Could it be true that Emotional Rags have a necessary place in the larger scheme of things? *What is their place in your place?* What is it that wakes you up? Are we where we are because of our obsessive, stubborn way of thinking?

There is a way out. But it will take a change in our thinking. It is the first step and the last step of the rest of our lives. Learning to live in our now moments gives us the strength we need to start the process of letting go of our old ideas and ways of thinking so that we can have new ways to process old worn out ways that never worked. The pushing of our life into our way of thinking starts the downward journey of letting go and letting God.

It may have been our holier, judgmental, and stubborn set of standards that kept us hidden and not available for any kind of healthy change. Well, that was our standard and that is the way we used to think. Everyone comes to the reality at some point that change, even unwanted change, is good.

So where is the help to see us through brutal unwanted change? Could it be that we really do have the answers within us? By asking for help, we have already put the healing and help we need into motion. By truly and sincerely asking for help, it will come. And so will the fear and the indecision and the doubt that we may not be hearing our inner soulful-self giving us the right direction. Just a little bit of trust and a dollop of faith will get us into motion. No, this will not be an instant oatmeal experience. It will take more than a quick three minutes before partaking but it will last a lifetime.

However, once nudged we feel as if part of the addictive burden is lifted. Our burdens are very heavy and keep us weighted down. Getting the nudge to change is one of the first weights that is lifted. What an exhilarating feeling.

NO WORRIES SPIRITUAL RICHES = BOUNTIFUL
There are plenty of Spiritual Riches to go around, and in order to keep what we have, there are some very basic requirements. Because we are here to share our good, we will find it somewhere in our consciousness. Automatically we will want to share our good fortune of how we found our Riches. That is with anyone who wants to listen. Not everybody will want to hear from us and that is okay.

There are many souls that need to stay in the negativity of their Rags in order to experience what it takes to have their Spiritual Riches. And we need to leave them alone until they are ready to share their journey. If we are the kind of person with all the answers for everyone else, we will find ourselves in not only our own lessons, but in the lessons of others.

In finding our answers to our own Emotional Rags we will find that sharing our success at healing our Rags to Riches is a great way to keep those Riches coming.

We can honestly share that our lives are much better and more fulfilled. We will have become more centered and feel much more positive about why we are even here.

One of the most powerful changes to occur is that we are no longer overreacting to the behavior of those we love or even to strangers. There is freshness in our souls and it feels good to breath in a new life that is not one of attachments or expectations. Addiction to anything that we choose is used to escape to attachments and expectations of others. Escape is a temporary cop-out and can never be the end of any story that we do not like in our life.

During a new found time of enlightenment, it is hard not to see a ONENESS in all things. Compassion is the key to seeing Oneness. When a person has been affected by life either personally or through the experience of being with another who has had to deal with an emotional trauma, it is much easier for us to see that similarities as opposed to judging another, is far easier...finally. This is a time when the understanding of a oneness that exists globally and universally would be hard to miss once we have experienced enlightenment on a spiritual level. It is a confirmation that we really are one.

Separation is no longer an option for us. We will find we are quick to note that we are judging others when we start to point fingers or tune in to judgments and assumptions. It becomes too uncomfortable to stay in that mode of thinking.

WHAT DOES IT TAKE FOR SEPARATION TO GO?

What does this mean personally for us? When do we finally start realizing the feeling of separation from God, Man, Plants, or Animals is gone? Life has changed. We are much more centered and comfortable in our own skin. Separation is no longer a natural state in our lives. We have come to recognize that the energy we are breathing is the same energy for all. The universe is a spiritual gold mine that belongs to everybody and everything. We are no longer noticing all the differences in others but are embracing the similarities.

Others, who have known us for a time, will be curious as to why we are so comfortable in our own skin.

Everyone seems to secretly want that kind of comfort; to feel a connection and a sense of belonging. It is for all and for the taking. Maybe that is why we need addiction to bring us to our knees. It changes what we look at because for the first time we are looking at us and how we need to change our thinking to change our lives. Many will travel on in their journey and not notice that connection and belonging is out there and it takes what it takes to wake us up.

EVERYONE GETS TO FIND THEIR WAY

Most of us want an opportunity to find a path of healing in specific areas of our lives. We may not call it healing but we know that we want a positive change. It could be in a job, a relationship, or a need for more money, more friends, and more direction.

Nothing has ever been hidden from us, yet nothing will appear until we are ready to accept the fact that we need help and that help has to be bigger and more powerful. Realizing the power that we do have access to actually lives within us.

This information and way of living has never been held hostage. Sages and Monks of old to present day have taught us that we can find the peace and enlightenment that lives within us. Seldom will we hear this truth from the pulpit. It takes away the control of telling us what to do and how to do it. It takes away a financial requirement and leaves a wide open commitment that now can come from the heart. These are more Rags that have detoured us from the Spiritual Path that is our own and has all the answers and all the direction we will ever need. The only thing this path does not have is the community of others and that is why attending a spiritual center of like minds can be so necessary and so invigorating. It charges us all up to champion each other's lives. What pure bliss this is and what joy it brings to us who want the comradery of others who are learning the path of Emotional Rags to Spiritual Riches.

Sages may sit in silence longer, and Monks may hibernate in the hills, but we too have the formula living within us of how to find our Spiritual Riches. Why would a loving God leave anyone out? Why would a Universe of perfection and synchronization not want us to have information on how to have a better life here? If we think not, then we will get what we think. How unfortunate for those of us who are not willing to change our thinking.

We will all have periods, in which we just cannot seem to get the formula of what will work with our inner selves. *We want what we want, and we want it now.* We often obsess over the Riches of material gain. *But are these the Riches we are really seeking? Or are they the ones that rust and fade? Or do they have a temporary life cycle? Are they timeless, traveling with us through eternity?*

The Riches we do discover may not show up as "instant oatmeal" ready in three to five minutes but they will be on time, and later, as we reflect back we will see that they will have arrived on "perfect time". The Universe knows our timing needs and all the others that are involved so everything requested is delivered appropriately on time at the right time. By listening, meditating, and through prayerful affirmation we will know we are experiencing our own "on time" moment. If we are present to the moments we are living in, we cannot help take the next step to show up to our still small voice that lives within. This is where our truth lives. This is another one of our biggest Spiritual Riches.

NO ONE IS LEFT OUT
No one is left out of a Rags to Riches experience. We are here to learn and this is the way we do it. Information is the key to our success at eliminating the Rags and embracing the Riches. Everyone wants the Riches but few are willing to do what it takes to accomplish this rightful inheritance.

There are others who will join in to be part of the gift of our Spiritual Riches. No pushing is allowed as it will not work anyway. It only complicates the rhythm which stalls the end results. Sometimes pushing even eliminates the right outcome at the right time. So don't push the water to get quicker results as we could easily drown in our own undertow.

Fortunately with others in the mix of our journey and its positive outcomes, we will find that Oneness is realized. Once we understand that we coexist with everyone always, our life improves and we all get better.

If we ever wonder if this new way of thinking is working as our life starts to improve, we only need to observe our own reality. The Riches start showing up and that will be proof enough that we are finally on track to a life abundant, focused, and representative of the best of why we are. Also just in seeing others manifesting a new way of living can be an awesome experience. There comes a certain feeling, a certain nudge that feeds our intuition with a zest and a quest for living a life that was trapped inside but is now out in the open and ready to bloom.

Some may say, "That can never happen to me." With the right thinking it not only will happen but it must happen. There is no way it cannot happen.

Our inner guides will bolt into action, and show us the way. We will be the difference, and then, we will be tuned in using for the first time our spiritual third eye: the eye of knowing that we know. Our third eye sitting in the center of our forehead has been closed until now. We have opened this eye by accessing our intuition to reveal how we see. In many cultures this is the Christ Consciousness or also referred to as the way of the Buddha to awareness.

Our guides will never let up on us, just as the God of our understanding never lets us go. There may be a waiting period, as we prepare for what is to come, but we will never be abandoned.

Sometimes in our human experience, we all slip back into old ways as we get closer to learning a new way of living. Let's face it, living in the NOW is not a way that many of us have experienced. Oddly enough, it seems that staying with our old ways is easier than change. However, once we experience all the energy-filled moments of the NOW, we will know that this is the way to live. This is what we had hoped for. And this is not something to let go of. Trying to stick with old ways becomes difficult and unsettling once we have had even a glimpse of what a NOW moment is and how it feels. So going back to our old ways is not a mistake, but a wake-up call to a new reality. *Is this not the part of the journey that gets our attention, and puts us back on track?*

SO WHAT IS IT...REALLY THAT WE ARE ASKING FOR?

Once we have good sound knowledge of what we are asking for as we journey down our road to accomplish our next right thing, what is it that we have asked for, and what are we seeking? Once we know what we are seeking we may find the Universe is not quite as forgiving when we return to an old, outdated way of living. That thinking is our past. It no longer works even in dysfunction. Discomfort sets in and we are uncomfortable. By being gifted with healing our Rags and enjoying our Riches we have joined a new dimension of a life of personal service. We are now present to all that we are and all that shows up to us in our daily lives. We become connected in a way that we have never been before. In addition, it no longer takes an extended time and/or multiple lessons to figure it all out. The discomfort of not showing up to what we know works now, becomes our best motivator to keep us moving. The Universe stops us much more quickly when we continue to repeat unhealthy behaviors.

This is an emotional rag that got the penicillin. We healed our rag, and we would have to work very hard to get the entire rag back. Even our egos have little to chatter about once we have conquered a lesson. We are no fun to mess with anymore. Our Now messages are receiving direct, pointed messages that let us know to resume our path and how to stay on track. *All in all, this is good.* We will no longer have the luxury to sit in old learned lessons long. There will be many indicators, out of the blue, to put us back on track.

Once we realize that we are not doing things the same old way, we actually attract like-minded souls to join us in completing our journey.

WE DO GET TO MANIFEST WHAT WE WANT

Everything we want and need can manifest through our thought processes. That means that if we have good thoughts or bad thoughts, we do get to have what we think. We live in a positive Universe. What we think becomes a positive to our lives. If we are thinking inspirationally we receive inspiration and manifestation. If we are doom and gloom and full of fear, that too becomes a positive in our life and we manifest the doom and gloom. The only requirement is quite simple if we want to manifest our good. Staying focused with good intention puts us into a thought process that already knows that our good is here. Our good is acknowledged and we know that it will continue to unfold right on time. We always have an inner power to make something happen, and that is why we need to monitor our thoughts. We are a magnet to thoughts. Our thoughts are who we are and what we become. We manifest within us all the time. What are we thinking today? What are we willing to listen to today? And are we ready to start being an observer of our own thoughts?

THE UNIVERSE ONLY KNOWS POSITIVES

So to reiterate, a positive universe only know positives; meaning that our thoughts, regardless of what we are thinking, remain a positive flow of co-creative connected energy; to re-emphasize the point - we get what we think in some form or another.

BEING TUNED IN TO OUR THOUGHTS
IS A LEARNED BEHAVIOR

It could be said that a wise person, who is careful with his or her words and thoughts, will be manifesting the wisdom and the good that they are thinking. It sounds easy but to be wise is to live long enough to learn that wisdom comes from mistakes and a great deal of experience. By observing our thinking patterns are learned wisdom and the key to catching the truth. Observing our thoughts makes sure that before a good thought eludes us with a brazen off the cuff remark of an unhealthy ego, we catch the remark that wants to put us into a fearful state and take away the freedom we are learning to manifest. The wisdom in the lesson of learning to listen to our soulful selves provides us the inward guidance that we receive from a Power greater than ourselves. Thus we are able to observe and to have our positive thoughts without losing them. Once we are the observer, we start giving ourselves first... the gift of manifesting which begins a process of sharing our gifts and giving them away unconditionally. We are finally connected to our true soulful selves, transparent, authentic and whole.

ANSWERED PRAYER IS ALREADY
KNOWING IT IS ANSWERED

Most of us, who have come to believe that we are spiritual beings, living an earthly life, have experienced the power of prayer. Many of us feel we know how to ask for what we need; but with the power of prayer and access to our Spiritual Riches, there is another step that assures our success. We would be good to affirm that the prayer has already been answered, and then let it go, knowing that the God of our understanding will manifest this request at the right time, in the right place, and with the right people involved. As we affirm our prayers, by knowing that they have been answered, we allow our thoughts of good intentions to manifest with patience. Our lives are no longer based on the "Instant Oatmeal" requirement. This requirement never works anyway. The simplicity of knowing that our thoughts are prayers will help us listen to what we are saying. This is just one more way to tether the ego, and observe our prayers. The ego untethered will want to steal our prayers of knowing that what we need has already been gifted.

Changing our thinking patterns is the biggest ongoing gift we can acquire. We will come to know that our old ways of life have imprisoned our true and authentic selves. We are signed up to be students who never stop learning. In this process of learning, we begin to reach our highest levels of Spiritual awareness in this lifetime. How comforting to know that when we leave this life and go onto the next, we have accomplished a more Christ-like consciousness or Buddha-like acceptance of enlightenment.

OUR BIG STUFF DEPENDS ON WHAT WE NEED TO LEARN

It is definitely a process to be in this thing called life. Some of us show up for our big stuff, and some of us wait until later. But, in the end, no matter how long it takes, whether this life or the next, we will all be in need of addressing our stuff.

We can choose to do our best or learn to attempt our best over and over again. Some of us need the repetition, while others want to move on quickly after a lesson is achieved. It doesn't matter how we individually get there because we are all ONE in all things. We are yin and yang. We give and take. We come to understand that being alive in this lifetime is an opportunity to become more of who we are. We will evolve, if we do the next right thing in this lifetime. If we do not, it is still not over...the Fat Lady has not yet sung. Her vibrato is unrelenting throughout eternity. In essence the song is never over.

We get a choice to view lessons as either good or bad. It matters little why or where these lessons come from. We still have a choice. Truthfully, we are all about having choices. Depending on how we have addressed and changed our thinking patterns, our similar situations, and old lessons may keep coming up. They may also grab our attention as many times as necessary, until we make the choice to heal or not to heal.

ADDICTION CURES A LESSON OR PUTS IT ON HOLD

There is no drug, no amount of alcohol, and no addiction out there that will allow us to hide our lessons, and true selves for long. We will be put on notice with a form of physical and/or emotional pain. This emotional rag is our opening to address our soul. Every soul is alike in that it has the potential to have, do, and be everything it is here to accomplish. If we die from addiction, we die with lessons still to be learned.

There may have been a time when we were allowed to check out, while still under protection of our consequences, but with a wake-up call of addiction, of any kind, there comes a day when it stops working. And, no matter how hard one tries to escape the soul's journey through addiction, surrender is the only spiritual richness that will save us from this emotional rag. Our old behaviors are worn out, and no longer work. *Not anymore.* We have crossed the line, and now feel the pain, which hopefully brings us to our senses. If not, we die as a result of not being able to release our addiction.

GOOD AND BAD CHOICES ARE NOT
A CONCEPT, BUT A CHOICE

We find ourselves nudged by a God of our understanding. We are nudged by our intuitive thoughts, our guides, and our angels. We get nudges from loved ones who have gone on ahead of us and are now with us in Spirit.

WAKE UP…IT'S TIME TO WAKE UP…BUT WILL WE?

We get nudged. And it happens to wake us up with whatever it takes to help us come into a NOW reality of where we are in our lives and what needs to change. We are being asked to surrender for our own good and the good of why we are here at this time on the earth. This is not an easy or planned surrender. It is our last breath before change. It is our only hope of survival. The choice is ours to make. Once decided, our real work of showing up has just begun. We are in a rebirthing process, even in our discontentment, and our willingness most often is to not yet be willing. It may take a couple more times of extreme pain, before we stay fixed firmly on the knees of surrender.

Upon readdressing our old life through surrender, and working on letting go of Emotional Rags, we become ready to accept our Spiritual Riches. They can come to us freely and with ease if we have really learned the finesse of letting go. But for most of us, it takes a while to understand the letting go process. It can only be done in the moment…and it takes thousands of moments of practice to finally give our lives to a loving God of our understanding. We were born of spirit so we have always had a spiritual beginning. It may have been a hesitant part of us to recognize as our lessons sometimes seem to block our spiritual side. We are the cause. Therefore, we create the effect of everything we do.

There are times in our stubbornness to change, when we by- pass intuition. Our intuition is our one source of the God within that will give us the answers we are seeking.

WHO WANTS TO BE A MARTYR…WE ALL DO, SOMETIMES!

We would rather put all of our energy into ignoring the Emotional Rags we are dragging with us. Silently and painfully like a martyr, we accept the

Emotional Rags, and carry them, as if we were victims of circumstance. And, we are…our own circumstances. Our dramas hit heights that are obvious to all but oblivious to us. We are wearing life, as if we were pushing a mountain that will not budge, or wearing spandex two sizes too small. We have not found loose garments that allow us to flow with the "ebbs and flows" of our lives. We are right until we are not. We are not present to anything, until we are. Our unhealthy chattering egos drown out all messages of well-being until we shut them down, and learn how to send them away on a moment's notice.

Our valiant victim-hoods, we own for as long as we choose to live in a world of separation. With our chins jutting out in defiance, we conclude that we are here to live out our drama and fears. What a pity party we have created for ourselves, yet how stubborn we are when it comes to changing our thinking patterns, so that our chins drops to a normal, comfortable position. Only then a smile can emerge.

No matter how we live…happy or defiant, depressed or fearful, alone or boisterous, we will always be the stars of our own shows. There is no one that has the exact same entrances and exits as we do. We write our own scripts, we are the directors, making changes, and we sponsor ourselves (or choose not to), and then, we live out our Emotional Rags until we come to the conclusion that we are ready for our Spiritual Riches. We may have doubts and fears, but being a "Doubting Thomas" will prevent us from moving to the next level. In the end, we are granted every opportunity possible to embrace all the spiritual richness known to man. We take what we need, and leave the rest. Our inner guide is the message giver as to what we need to carry on the life we have chosen. We definitely are the "choosers" of our destinies, and like it or not, we are living what we chose right NOW.

If we have chosen to live our lives at a level of low energy, our outward actions will tell our stories to the world. We tell the world, without even having to mutter a word, as to just how badly we think we have it. We ask others by our actions, to watch us to take a look, feel our pain, and be the one to sit through our Rags. Some bathe in self-pity by sharing the albatross we have willfully tied around our necks. The high drama is apparent. In fact, we are only attracting high drama. The only ones listening to our woes are the ones who dramatize along with us about their own lives. It definitely becomes a choice of consciousness or unconsciousness. But, we are the ones that make that choice.

IT CAN BE VERY RISKY TO BE INVISIBLE: RISKY TO US

Then, there are those of us who hide in our emotions by staying noticeably quiet. We choose to be stealthy. We are watchers, who stay in the background with little to say, as being invisible allows us not to participate in life. *What risk is there to being invisible?* Being invisible is like a groundhog, without his shadow. We pop up occasionally but we retreat even faster into our hole. No one gets to decide how to love, or honor a person who is invisible. They bring neither goodness nor badness to the table of life. But, someday, when they see their bump and run approach to life, they will find that others will stop paying attention. And yet, no one is ever left out when discovering the soul's journey, and the reason why we are here. We can ignore it, but time will reveal it, even if we choose not to share it.

So, the time comes when the invisible is very visible. God IS and God IS everywhere and our Oneness to our higher selves has to emerge at some point. The soul will emerge, and when that happens, there will be an emergence that will define the lifetime of our souls. However, there will be those who will have to emerge in another lifetime. This lifetime is getting them ready. Quiet people who are contemplative are not the ones who are invisible. If they are in a contemplative state which is quiet in this lifetime, they will also be preparing but for a much bigger role of teaching and giving away spiritual gifts in another lifetime.

Egos can disguise our souls with various personalities and masks. The tendencies to drink and do drugs, along with any other kind of addictive behaviors, can sidetrack our Emotional Rags, but in the end…we must emerge to the God of our understanding, no matter what we call this Higher Being. Our higher consciousness always wins, either in this lifetime or the next.

Addictions have a place for a certain amount of time. For example, a person needing to hold on to Emotional Rags, in the form of addictions, may do so because of a lack of trust and faith in something greater than themselves. These souls seek out anything that is mind and mood altering. They do not want a conflict with their egos and hearts but that is exactly what happens. And, when the battle begins, as it always does, the addiction can quiet our hearts, fill our heads with fear, and leave us empty of all purpose. No decisions are made. No wealth of Spiritual Riches is received.

We shop until we drop, drink until we pass out, drug ourselves into "La-La Land," eat until we can't move, and/or use sex as a temporary fix, but the fix is always short - temporary. And, then, the day comes, when it is no longer a suitable "fix." But, until then, from one fix to the next, we seek anything and everything that allows us not to think, listen, or heal.

Our defiance is the emotional rag used to score our next quick fix. Addictive behaviors work for a while, but eventually become noticeably tempered with varied degrees of "bottoming out." This is needed to get our attention. There are the few who are able to catch themselves before they lose everything. But even in a high bottom catch, specific wake up calls are evident at every juncture.

Many have never awakened from this insanity; rather, they have simply lost everything, and then died. Sometimes, death is their way of transitioning out of this life, and other times they die, while they are living. They are walking death without the mental capacities to participate in life.

The finale of facing addiction is an end of life experience. Our lives are never the same once we know what we need to know about addiction and why we are at low ebb in our lives. And hopefully, it is at the finale of addiction that the birth occurs. We produce the "PHOENIX RISING EFFECT." And, out of the ashes comes our rebirth…a living breathing resurrection that is seen by all. It is a starting over point. We are not only starting over but we are blessed with starting again; this time we have the willingness to change the way we think so that our lives rebirth into why we are here. We have a soulful life to live, complete with a contract to fulfill. Our old lives are left in the ashes. Our new lives have taken flight. We have found our first set of Spiritual Riches. There is sobriety, serenity, hope and courage to fearlessly change.

Our nirvana, our peace, lives within us. Our re-birthing at selected times in our life can validate this truth. When our Emotional Rags hold us captive we are kept from the lives we are here to discover. But as long as we are here and even if our lives look like a disaster, we are alive and there is time for changing our thinking to change our lives. For those who want to make quantum leaps of change, they will have the opportunity. We all get it. Sometimes we just do not know it or hear it.

For those who seem to not get it, our job is to know that they are not ready or not willing and that the journey they are on is none of our business. Just as we will get where we are going at the right time, so will they. Judging others does not correct behavior or difficult lives. It just adds to the challenge and many times will not permit souls to begin the healing process.

A Higher Power is a High Watch Energy Field that knows us before and after our tribulations with emotional bottoms. The Riches remain protected and ready to distribute as we start our healing process. We are never alone. We just are not aware of the help constantly circling us.

Is there a special time to address our emotional bottoms? There is not a right or wrong time under Universal law. The time is right when we are right with what we need to do. The right time is whenever the decision is made. It is just not possible to be in the wrong place when we are ready. As is the Universe, we are always right on time to our life, good or bad. *We will have choices.* Well, whichever way we choose to go, the decision will remain positive for where we are with our growth. We will receive the positive or negative results that we have chosen to experience. What we think is what we will ultimately end up receiving. With manifestation for the good we have done as we align our lives with Spirit, we will get the memo that it is our time to move forward toward our greater good. And, interestingly enough, our greater good may be in the form of a lesson that teaches us that we need to succeed in our quest for Spiritual Riches. Substance abuse, in all forms, will no longer take the pain away. In addition, alcohol, prescription drugs, sex, food, or whatever, will work for us until we find a bigger-than-life brick wall. *The course has been run.*

ESCAPING ADDICTION COMES TO AN END…
The time spent in the escape of addiction can be over. It no longer takes away the pain of our past, present and future fears. This temporary fix has become just that - positively temporary.

Opportunities are now upon us to change, to change our thinking patterns which change our behavioral patterns. And, when this occurs, many of us will have changed just one thing. *Everything.* Who would have guessed? Who wants to, at the beginning of such a journey?

There are those who say, "I do not have an addiction. I just need to calm down. I will change what I do to something less addictive." But, in addiction, anything that is mind-altering can get out-of-control. Mind altering is anything that takes us out of our NOW and puts us into obsessive/compulsive thinking using something that stops our rational good thinking. Anything that stops us from hearing the truth about ourselves is what we are trying not to think about.

Therefore, it is good to understand that many of us are addicted to something. If we pick the right and healthy addictions, it will be in our best interests. If we are not with mind and mood altering behaviors, a healthy addiction can manifest in the way we treat and do for others. We may find a passion which is another purpose for our lives while we are here. In this passion we may find that we are totally consumed. The difference is that when we have accomplished a purpose, we will know to stop. We will be done. There will be no withdrawals, health issues, or a need to live in the past of whatever we choose to do for the greater good. We sometimes call this a type "A" personality. We will find that our addictive goods, in a certain area of our expertise, are beneficial to all. But of course balance is always the preferred way to be if at all possible. When switching addictions, we can find something that is much more self-serving than mind-altering drugs. The goal is to use those passions to act out our addictive natures.

THERE WILL ALWAYS BE A TIME
WHEN WE ALL SURRENDER

Everyone has a point of surrender, so that they become the best that they can be. Hard as it is for some, and easier for others, everyone in this lifetime learns how to surrender to someone, or something. Once we have tapped into our higher conscious selves, we become "teachable" to why surrender is such a powerful tool. It may have been that up until now, we were not open to being teachable. Surrender affirms lives that not only bring the promises of spiritual richness, but also the success living within us. Our Emotional Rags have brought us a long way at this point. Rags are great teachers. We are beginning to fully understand.

DON'T WE ALL OVERDOSE OVER
SOMETHING AT SOMETIME?

With eventual certainty we all succumb to our own self-induced overdoses. It seems a necessary process in our life cycles to find out what works, and what does not. We live with the "yin and yang," the ups and downs, and many opportunities that are not just by chance, which enable us to access our greater higher selves.

Brought to our knees by total realization, we finally understand why we are so sick of being sick and tired. Some will say: "A bell goes off;" "A light goes on;" "A click in our consciousness snaps us out of a foggy reality that we will never forget." All addictions are usually patient and many times silent prior to a wake-up call to heal. The wake-up call can be devastating or subtle but everyone eventually gets it. Caught in the moment of truth, there is always that moment of no safe escape for any form of addiction. It is time to address our addictive Rags and then it will be time to experience our Spiritual Riches.

Exposed, and in the light of the truth of who we really are, and who we have become, addiction ends up begging to be healed. It no longer works for us.

When the time is up, the time is up!

Hiding is no longer an option.

It no longer works.

Spiritual energy is circling and is now ready to save us with our own willingness. Spirit has waited for us to be ready for a new way of thinking which produces a new way of living.

Help has always been on the way, but were we ready to be on the way? We are never ready to cure an addictive nature until we are ready. It is a new way. It will become our new way. It belongs to everyone who is ready. And away we go.

Emotions run rampant. The ego wants to hold on tightly and not relinquish control. *Many ask, now what? What's next? How can I do this?* Suicidal thoughts fueled by the ego can add to confusion.

Letting the ego go means there will be all the mindfulness needed for the listening and receiving that is now needed. The powerful mind, the ego, is not related to a life of mindfulness – let alone listening and receiving.

Instead, the chattering ego likes to inundate a soul's addictive journey with thoughts of fear and doubt. The chatter leaves no room for peace. This is why meditation and quieting down is so important. The ego must be silenced for healing to begin.

But the soul has the capability of shutting down the ego. There is a life out there that is an easier softer way.

LIFE ON LIFE'S TERMS
Yes, there is life to live, on life's terms, bridges to cross, miles to run, and mountains to climb. That is what it takes. It becomes and really is a personal journey.

For all of us, and that means everyone, there is a small still voice that lives within us that will nudge us and remind us of who we really are. Finding that voice is not difficult once we learn the gift of shutting down and listening. That small still voice has nothing but positive affirmative messages. It comes from our heart and reminds us who really is in charge of our change.

There is hope for all of us. There is trust within us and it is a survival mode that carries us to the Highest Conscious levels where we will need to heal. Amazingly this healing and the way we heal lives within us and we will learn how to activate this beautiful power that lives within.

Hope and trust live within us, too. When we think we have an option of giving up...we do that until we remember we have a power greater than ourselves on our side standing by ready to carry us until we can get one foot in front of the other.

Fearful Emotional Rags feed on negativity and addictive thoughts. The Emotional Rags may even convince us that we are hopeless. A soul connected to our God Source does not know hopelessness. Acknowledging our Source and Supply along with hope is a prayer in action. Our thoughts become prayers and our prayers affirm hope.

Hope in the context we are speaking is an action step. Hope guided with trust and faith can do nothing but the next right thing in our healing process.

IS AN INTERVENTION AN ACT OF GOD?
Interventions can save a life temporarily, but not "fix" an addiction. Addictions do not want to be fixed. They have a life of their own and keep us jailed in an unhealthy ego that is afraid to let it go. Many think they cannot live without their addiction. But the truth is they are not living with it. The illusion of addiction saving someone from themselves is truly an illusion.

A person who has loved ones and family forcing an intervention is a risk to the addictive one. They are usually not ready even though they are hurting, experiencing loss, and ruining their ties with family, friends and their employment. But it can be at least a start to get their attention. The question still arises, are they ready to face their demons? Do they know how sick they are? Can they surrender...really surrender... to a program that will show them how to achieve sobriety? This kind of addiction is serious and pertains to drugs and alcohol that have taken away their life.

So, an intervention is not a "for sure" fix, but it may save a life and keep someone safe for the time being. There is always something learned in this process performed by loved ones to at least introduce a recovery program. At least they will realize that they are not alone. Any progress in changing addictive thinking, large or small, is good. And sometimes it may take years for that ah-ha moment to come. The timing is always right. The message will be heard when it is meant to be heard.

LOSING A LOVED ONE TO SUICIDE

What is there about this decision made by others who make a decision to commit suicide and not live out their lives? What were they thinking? Or more accurately, what were they not thinking? Will we ever know? Are we supposed to know what made them become so wounded that they saw no way out? We will feel the pain and the loss and think we know why but we never will know the intensity of such a decision. This is one more thing that is not ours to know.

We all have had some Emotional Rags and we will again. I was also not left out of the Emotional Rag of someone close to me committing suicide. If we never have to go through the things we go through we will never know the intensity of feelings for another. So by walking through a suicidal incident we may not know why, but we know more. We become part of the experience. We may even have clarity about why we could never do such a thing and still have the compassion for the one that did. I became one of those who learned compassion, sorrow, and confusion when my father took his own life.

So on a personal note, I would like to share a story about my dad who committed suicide. My dad, from as long as I can remember, was never quite right. He was high strung, nervous, and a chain smoker. He was always "right" at home and always "right" at work. When it came to our neighbors the family was not allowed to talk to them and he was mean and disgruntled to the point of sneering at them and swearing in the foulest language if he got the chance.

Was it because he was a small man, a wiry man, an insecure man that was fighting his own demons every day or was he just a dark evil person? He looked and sounded evil. But he really was not. He was a very gifted man but his gifts were exchanged for a bad temperament, violence with his family and rage with the world. What could have possessed him to have all that turmoil and ugly behavior? Once a handsome man, he became ugly early in his life, lost his teeth from gum disease, used pills to get up and pills to go to sleep with a side of alcohol. He was more than obsessive/compulsive as he had multiple addictions including perfectionism which only gave him very low self-esteem. What happened to this man that would verbally abuse, sexually abuse, and physically abuse his family? Why was he out of control? It was not until after his violent cross-over that I got the message. It came to me very clearly. His behavior stemmed from past behaviors that he had either experienced or engaged in. Being born to a French-Canadian father who beat him and beat the farm animals and rarely spoke, could have started the cycle. Maybe it was that he was the youngest of three, not expected, and much like his mother. There is always so much we do not know about a wounded soul even if it is a parent. But the truth he carried with him ever since I knew him was that he was a man full of fear, and rage. His anger showed itself in the way he talked, walked and engaged with anyone. His self-esteem seemed to be compensated with verbal and physical abuse to his family. husband. For better or worse it meant she was going nowhere. And with an eighth grade education, she had fears of her own as to how she would ever support herself and three young children.

If you were to ask people who knew our family they most likely would say that the family as a whole suffered severe abuse. This was especially so as we lived in close proximity to the neighbors as all the homes were close together and it was impossible to keep family business from being heard.

Especially so as my father would rage on for hours at a time. He had no respect for our neighbors and we were not allowed to talk to them. And there was no question that we were abused as children by a wounded, mentally ill parent. My job was to protect my mother...I did most of that by worrying, supporting her and going to bat for her. However, when could have or needed to go to bat for me, she could not. Her fear of my father was far to great to protect her children's interest when my father was on the war path abusing his family physically and verbally.

This man was so hurt that he hurt others all the time. He did not like anyone especially himself. He just was not comfortable in his own skin. And when the drugs and alcohol were added to the equation, all hell broke out and it was a very scary place to be: that 1949 Cape Cod on Shangri La Drive. It was no Shangri La.

What happened to him to bring out all this hate and self-loathing? It came with him from a brutal past. Some of which he grew up with and some of his own doing. He was involved in some secret organizations, the mafia, and who knows what else along the way. Why did he marry for the second time to a woman who was naive and willing to iron his underwear? Because he had full control over her and the three children they brought into the world. This was a man who deeply needed help but was not willing to admit that he had a problem. Instead he used addictions, all kinds of addictive behavior to mask and validate all of his inappropriate and hurtful behavior. And much of the hurtful behavior was not only to his family, neighbors, co-workers, but the worst pain was his own.

His addiction like all addictions was a progressive dis-ease to the body, mind and spirit. By the end of his life after a divorce from my mother, multiple mental institutions, the painful death of my brother that he could never deal with, he became sedated by doctors in a State Hospital until he was released to a half-way house a few years later. The State thought he was ready to live on his own so he was moved into to a large high rise with many people who were the same age. Some were troubled and some were not. It was low cost housing but clean and suitable for his now new home. It was close to a bar that he visited daily with his oxygen tank at home and at the bar where he was able to be truly wounded and let the people that came in daily and the bartender and wait staff know that he was pitiful because of what his family had done to him. He was already on medications for depression and anxiety and then his thirst for his daily alcohol was the topper. Being lonely and miserable, the bar was his sanctuary. He was not willing to change his thinking and because of that his life had gotten increasingly sad and lost.

His family of birth was afraid of his mental illness even though they had experienced it first-hand every visit we ever made to go see his family. They considered his mental illness and addiction a black mark on the family name. That in itself was a mental illness of not understanding his disease.

Fortunately, in today's world, that kind of archaic thinking is changing but mental illness is still not totally understood by families that are challenged. Education is the answer and the dialogue will continue to change over time.

During the end of my father's life, he committed suicide by jumping out of his apartment window. He jumped out of a 13-story building and because he always thought so tragically, it was no surprise that his memorial service fell on his birthday. He was 62 years old. It was the end of his lung disease. It was the end of the pills, the oxygen to help him catch his breath in between many cigarettes. No more drinking to remember or feel badly for the way things turned out. No more blaming his ex-wife and children for ending up institutionalized. No more mental illness to contend with… he was finally in a safe place. I think he had been looking for a safe place his whole life.

Of course there has always been the question of why? And the question of why not? What was left for him? My Dad was spiritually and emotionally bankrupt. His body was worn out and he was hardly able to move or breathe. But what gave him the courage to jump out of that window? Was the drinking and drugging not hiding his pain anymore? So as brutal as suicide can be, some people want to pull the plug on their own lives when there is nowhere else that they are willing to go to heal their intense pain.

On the day he committed suicide I was 1500 miles away yet I felt his fall and his body hit the ground. I was jolted. It was real and I knew it was one of my parents that were no longer with me.

I was on my way to grocery shop when a jolt of terror, intense energy, straight forward and incredibly strong went straight through me. I turned the car around and immediately went home. The telephone was ringing out the bad news that I already sensed. I knew that one of my parents had died.

I left that day for a funeral three days later. It was one of the saddest days of my life for all the reasons one would not expect to be.

I was stunned and saddened at all that was not left of my father's life. He had committed suicide long before the actual day that took his life. His lonely long days were spent in a local neighborhood bar, while his barmates listened to his stories of woe. He filled them with his grief at what his family had done to him to bring him to this forlorn end of his road. He was alone even with four barstools on each side filled. His victimized life shared in a bar never did heal him but it empowered the friends he made to give him the compassion he had been seeking his whole life.

The abuse to our family I later learned was an opportunity to let go and forgive him. It was the only thing that worked for me so that I could have a life free from repeating, or living with the abuse that I had grown up with. Forgiveness is very powerful.

With my father, it was never an option to forgive himself because he had convinced himself that he was right about everything. He just never thought to want to bring a different thought or to bring a different conclusion to this life. Instead he lived a very painful, sad, and lonely life right up to the end of his tragic end. Possibly that moment of taking his own life was the recognition that he had done some wrong and ending his life was his way of stopping the pain of having to live with so many thoughts that would not let him be free. I will never know but I am content to know that he has a better life on the other side. He is healing.

When he jumped out of that window, he was letting go of resentments, judgments, hate, fear, and the loss of an entire lifetime of joy that he could have had. What does it take for us to see ourselves? Why do some of us have to wait so long or die tragically from a disease related illness to addiction? It takes what it takes. But life is never ending and with a new beginning my father will have the opportunity to heal the wounds that took his life long before he fell to his death. So where was God when all this happened? Right with my Dad as always. But he was unaware until he crossed over.

DAD COMES TO ME IN A DREAM…

It was not too long after he had been cremated and his ashes were put on his brother's grave that my dad came to me in a dream. I find it will help the reader if I share a little more about the truth of this man. He loved gardens and especially rock gardens. He had a feeling for the flowers and for trees. And as I mentioned previously he came into this this earth with many talents to share.

I had a dream that I was building him a rock garden on a sand dune on Lake Michigan. Dad loved the lake and loved rock gardens as he had built one in our back yard. People would slow down and complement him as he was working on it. He hauled beautiful rocks home and strategically placed them in this masterpiece he was creating.

In the dream it was a sunny, hot day and the sky was as blue as his penetrating eyes had been. He was at the top of a staircase that I had finished directly in the middle of the rock garden. It mirrored what he had built in the home I grew up in. He was coming towards me. I was planting flowers for him and terracing the garden just like he had done. It was a beautiful garden and I can still see everything from this dream very vividly. I could see the mums, phlox, the scattering of decorative vines, beautiful flowering bushes, and an array of other artifacts such as bird baths and flamingos. Yes, they were pink.

When he had made his self-decided transition, my first thought was that he would haunt me. The physical and verbal abuse had been so hard to bear as a child; as an adult the judging and verbal abuse calmed down if he did drugs which kept him quieter.

So when I saw him at the top of the stairs I was a little unnerved in my dream and said nothing. I was prepared for more verbal abuse. But in this very visual dream in color, he came to me, knelt down beside me and said, "I'm sorry, Dave." That was all. Nothing more. I remember turning to him and feeling deep compassion and I said, "Everything is going to be alright now." At that moment it was as if I had forgiven him for everything. I felt free with deep compassion and full of a love that was overwhelmingly sweeping over me. It was a direct message and indication that I would not have to be concerned about his haunting me. My amends came in the form of forgiveness and he too was taking care of what he needed to do before he moved on. I no longer had ill feelings for him. I felt only a deep compassionate love. As the dream came to a close I remember him grabbing a small shovel and helping me finish my tribute garden to him that was given without even knowing that he would show up in a dream.

It has been many years since I have healed and I am very free of those childhood and early adult years and his inability to love me. He did the best he could for whatever torment he was going though. I try to remember he did make progress in this lifetime and my lessons with him are over. I did make one commitment to myself and I have kept it. I promised myself that if I came in contact with anyone like him that I would be loving and compassionate. I have done so.

SHARING HELPS OTHERS

There is no longer a need to talk about what happened to me in my childhood, unless it is to help another person in a similar situation. I trust and feel deep in my heart center that my Dad is being prepared to re-enter for a lifetime that will address the demons that took his life in this lifetime.

Intuitively I have been gifted with knowing that my Dad's inability to address his sickness was the cause of his demise. My sadness cannot change anything that happened in those active years of his mental illness. But his life and the loss of it before he even left have taught me to be willing.

I have learned that we cannot be ready when we are never wrong and live with an illusion of always being right. Without my commitment to being an authentic, transparent person, to the best of my abilities, I too could lose my life while I am still alive. I want to be able to know when I need to surrender. My Emotional Rags are my opportunity to change. I want to live my story recognizing that I am perfect and whole and willing to return to this truth with the help of a God in my life that already knows my good. Thank you God for letting me have what I need to heal if I want it. My life as a spiritual warrior is not a life based on doctrine and someone else telling me how to believe. I have that within. But tell me what you did to find your center and I will be all ears even when I think I know. There are many paths to the Universal Energy. I am interested in all of them and will share as much as I know with whom ever wants to listen. I keep healing because I keep giving away my experiences, strength, and hopes. I keep healing because I love you, and I love me and the life we are all here to experience. Heaven has made it to my doorstep and I never had to leave the house. This would be my hope for all humanity. I know it is a process but with willingness we just can't miss the spiritual richness because we gave up, being a victim of our own self-made circumstances.

SPIRITUAL RICHES ARE THE MIND
OF GOD WHICH WE ARE

What does it mean to have the mind God? We may have been taught that a statement such as having the mind of God would be considered blasphemous. The truth is there is no separation between God and ourselves. There is no separation unless we separate. Spiritual Richness is the energy and mind of God. We have it all. Yes, it does take Rags to get there but they are the Emotional Rags we need to learn in this lifetime. What if we were to say thank you for an Emotional Rag that could change our thinking and change our life?

God IS. We ARE connected to the God who is everywhere. This energy knows nothing about boundaries when it comes to us having it all. The ALL of God is only good. The only boundaries are the ones we create and we can be very good at that. When the ego has its grip, the mind of God that lives within is lost in a muddle of multiple untrue messages. Living in a denial of a lesson prolongs what we are really here to do. Learn our lessons, live freely and we get to give away our gifts. In fact, we want to give them away because of the passion that surrounds them.

We have our gifts upon our entry to this beautiful earth. But the onion must be peeled layer by layer so we can get to our core good after we have addressed all the layers that need to be healed. Our job is to find our gifts by feeling what they are. We will know because they will feel like a natural part of us coming through intuitively. Then we proceed and give them away by showing up to our life and the lives of others with the messages that will give others their needs. If we do this, we are assured of keeping them.

Our guides, Angels and loved ones who have gone on are ready and willing to help us maneuver through this earthly maze of learning our lessons to give us the freedom to move into the real reason we are here. This real reason does not mean we are to be anything but ourselves. We will be standing in a new classroom every day. What is it that you would like to learn today? Which classroom would be most valuable? What is it that will heal your troubled soul? Once the human soul knows it lives within, our last action step is simply to listen to that still small voice and follow the messages that come through.

WHAT IS THE NAME OF OUR SOURCE AND SUPPLY?

We may call our Source and Supply God, Buddha, Christ, a Mountain or anything that speaks to a loving presence bigger than ourselves. If we stumble over the word God because of its misuse in our religious upbringing, there are many other words that mean the same thing; or we can even make one up so that we have a direct connection with the energy we seek.

Most people agree that there is a POWER greater than ourselves; a power greater than ourselves that wants us to have all that we need in this lifetime. Because if we do believe, we are part of the whole and we are giving away the good. Why wouldn't the God of our understanding want us to have his gifts? Our lives become simpler, easier, and more meaningful to all we touch. We were born into this lifetime with a purpose. The only souls that stay unhappy are the ones that do not recognize their value and purpose. However, there is such a small veil between knowing and not knowing. Everyone gets to see through the veil either through an experience of an emotional rag or an intuitive thought. Then the choice to change our thinking to change our lives becomes real. So what is it going to take for us personally to let this happen so we get our opportunity to have it all?

SELF-CARE POINTS THE WAY... TO FINDING THE WAY
Self-care at this point is essential for us to start being ready, able and willing to realize that something bigger than ourselves has never gone away and is only a breath inhaled to connect us with the ENERGY that has been with us for our entire journey.

Self-care is not tricky. We just have to do it. Are we willing to look at our mind, body and spirit and let it work together by listening to what the mind and the body need to achieve optimum results? The ego would like to introduce daily many levels of fear to keep us from hearing the real messages. But if we ask a direct question and then listen, we will start the process rolling and we will find ourselves getting help from all areas and sources. This may sound hokey to those who have never tried this approach. It may sound unreal. To be out there. To be New Age. How badly will we have to hurt to start getting just a sense that this is true? Or that maybe if we tuned into this simple age old formula that we might get results? For some it will take a tragic circumstance in their life. If we are at least willing to entertain an attempt the determination can be made after we get brave enough to just try. At this juncture of just asking, the healing has already begun.

So by asking a Higher Power, a God of our understanding, we are finally willing to recognize that the help we need is out there. We will be immediately supported. We are supported even without asking at certain times. But asking gives us the connection and then affirming that we have this connection puts it into play. Asking is the way of bringing a quicker and more recognizable response to our needs. The Spiritual Riches will pour over us through the vehicle of books, people, places, and our own intuitive new thought. Answers will come falling around us like the warmth of a wool overcoat in the middle of a sub-zero icy winter. We are loved until we can love ourselves and we begin to really feel it. We are guided until we do show up naturally.

In a quiet moment of our own truth we will recognize that we have been cuddled and protected but yet still have experiences we need to have so that we can grow into being the best of who we are. At this point for many of us we will access for the first time a sense of self-love, a recognizable support from many different sources. We are on our way out of Emotional Rags to Spiritual Riches.

NO ONE ELSE CAN DO OUR WORK...IT IS UP TO US

No one else can do our work. The work we need to do is ours and ours alone. This is a custom job and we must take this healing walk on our own with the help of having someone do it for us. Is it really work? Is there fear in moving forward? Will it be hard? All of these questions have the answer already in our mind's eye. Those answers are up to us to make them positive affirmations or we can choose the tired negative way we have been going because we have thought it to be easier. It has been a thought of ease only because we do not know another way. The way we can do our work to make our life better is the softer easier way. But we will have to decide on how we are thinking to get that positive assessment of the healing process we are embarking on.

We could actually stop ourselves by deciding it is too hard before we even try. The next stop is hitting a bottom in our life that will get our attention. Not to worry, if the first bottom does not bring us to our knees, there will be more until we are exhausted from hitting the bottom. We do not have to but some of us will not give in to having a life free of Emotional Rags, full of addiction. We would rather fight the right way so we can keep living the wrong way. At this level we could finally die of mental exhaustion or a body that no longer can hold up under the misuse. But if we so choose to live a new way without addictions we will find ourselves in the power of the greatest power there is and we will be rebirthing our lives.

Deep in our consciousness, a still small voice of hope will continue to gently remind us that there is something bigger than we are. But what if we are so low at the start of this new journey? How can someone feel so low and still hear that small still voice that is calling out to us as we wait for our answers? How can we listen when we are still stuck in our own muck? Do we start by trying…or do we just show up to the next right thing in our lives? Do we practice our new way of doing things or do we get complacent and stop trying after a week or two or when life throws us another curve ball? When we start to count on something bigger than ourselves to get us where we are now going, we do this not by trying but by being…in the moment. We become willing to meditate instead of medicating. We are never forced to heal. But when we decide to take that quantum leap, the old ways of hiding and disguising our feelings do not work anymore. Our temporary fix is no longer our short-term ace in the hole.

TIME IS ALWAYS ON OUR SIDE…ALWAYS

Time IS and is always on our side. We are never in the wrong moment, but we may be in the wrong awareness or lack thereof. With trust, there is a deep knowing that there is a way to find our answers. And trusting is the way we show ourselves and the God of our understanding that we too are doing our part. As we recognize that we are one with the God of our understanding, there is a trust that God will help those of us who are ready and that God must trust us enough that we will come to the point of being ready. A very old saying my Mother used to say was, "God helps those who help themselves." I found it to go a little deeper. I do help myself to serenity, non-judgment, loss of fear, and having the things in my life to make it easier. It occurred to me that my loving abundant God that made this deliciously abundant Universe was not a God of lack. If we are One with God then we are One with all he has and we may "help ourselves".

THE EARTH, STARS, AND PLANETS
ARE MINE TO ALIGN WITH

As the planets move in perfect synchronicity, we too join in the perfect timing of the Universe. When we are out of our own orbit, we will be unable to move freely and experience the magnificence that we are born into. However, at the moment of realization, clarity of purpose comes through in our NOW. We will see what we need to see to come to the reality of living with Spiritual Riches. The ONENESS that has always been available to us is directly in front of us. We will be back in orbit circling the Universe in our own creative positive energy that is connected to a Higher Source. These are the times of progress because we are co-creating with God. The time comes. The time will be right. One may ask, "When are we out of orbit?" Just check on how you are feeling, coping and tuned in. Are you agitated, sleepless, full of anxiety? If so, you are out of orbit.

EVERYONE GETS A MOMENT OF TRUTH LISTENING OR NOT

The moment of truth shines through at some point, perfectly on time, and any emotional rag that we have so attentively been attached to turns into a risk as it cannot compete with Spiritual Riches. It is the ego and our true Source and Supply that have the war, but eventually the good (our Source and Supply) always wins. We may have felt at one time or another that we would never ever be okay, that we would never have a chance for the peace and the Spiritual Riches we yearned for. We may have thought we were not good enough or healthy enough or that our hair had to be blonde. Whatever we were thinking in this way was just one more Emotional Rag ambushing our ability to experience Spiritual Riches. No one is ever left out once they have surrendered to a change in thinking. The faith and the trust in the process… is our beginning. Up until now, for many of us, listening was our main option. But how can we listen if we are a doubting Thomas? How can we listen if we are full of fear?

PROGRESS NEVER MEANS WE KNOW IT ALL

We knew it all and yet…we didn't; we believed we did and so we faked it. Rolling around aimlessly was no longer viable. We were called on our shit, and it was time to change. If the time is right and we are really ready to make the commitment to tune in with the communication that works with the God of our understanding; which is to allow change to bring us to our senses, it will happen. We will finally not only want to change but we will *become* the change.

Not all of us have to have the requirement of hitting a horrific emotional bottom. A bottom of losing almost everything except our life to get our attention. Many of us do not have to lose everything to get our attention. But those of us with High Bottoms and still have our homes, cars, jobs, and look like our lives are going along well, will face another ego dilemma. Oddly enough, in both a low and a high bottom the Ego will love telling us that we are not that bad. We really do not have to change that much. We are not like the rest of the world who are changing their thinking to change their lives. But the common denominator for all change is that everyone must do one thing, no exceptions. That one thing is to change one thing... EVERYTHING. It sounds like a tall order, but those of us who have changed everything have realized what that means. A change in thinking automatically changes everything. However, change of habits, change of friends and so forth are all part of this equation. It may take some time, but it will happen as we change our thinking. We actually will no longer understand or value what we thought we did in our old friends that we had attracted. Gratefully they were a segment, an important segment in this part of our journey.

RESULTS OF CHANGE HAPPEN WHEN
WE CHANGE OUR RULES

Those of us who still are not willing...will be the ones that insist on doing almost everything the same old way, think the same old thoughts, and keep showing up to the same old things. And we are the ones who will continue to get the same old results. Yet, as odd as it sounds, we will be right on time with our journey. We are not ready yet to move into a higher level of consciousness. Our ego still has control and will keep us going in the same direction until we are faced with the next crisis. At the point of again finding out that our thinking has brought us down a similar path as before, we will be at that juncture in our road again. Once again we will be able to make a more positive connected choice that excludes the ego. Thankfully there is no judgment as we attempt to grow. Our self-judgment is more than enough for us to handle. Hopefully we can take a breath and at least observe that there are changes to be made. This is the first step to becoming willing.

In a world of Spiritual Riches, the change in us has already occurred. We are attracting change when we are ready and with change come the Spiritual Riches we intuitively know in a still quiet moment belong to us. But they require us to be a gate keeper and protect them yet give them away. Our thinking is producing change and positive results. What we think and do is where we are in that moment. How we live is what is right with us in the NOW moment. We can change and will change many times in our life. As the Gate Keeper and the Spiritual Warrior on the High Watch, our job is to keep the changes coming and let the Universe manifest the best of who we are. We just show up!

SOME LOSE IT ALL AND SOME DO NOT...WHY?

There is no reason to lose it all if we catch the problems we are having in a timely manner. The lessons that we are in and trying to change may still remain difficult, but if we catch the drift of what is holding us back, we may not have to lose as much as some do.

Fortunately, there are some who do not need to totally bottom out for the Universe to get their attention. People with High Bottoms do not lose it all. But this does not discount the fact that there is willingness and commitment needed to be a high priority to get the personal work done. Life is really never lost but it is over in the way it used to be. Reverting back no longer works. We have 'way too much information and once the information comes to us there is less tolerance from all energies to let us go back in one of our unhealthy patterns. So let us check your stats...how and what are we thinking today?

WE LIVE IN A POSITIVE UNIVERSE...
EVERYTHING IS POSITIVE

It may sound odd to think that everything is positive...everything! But we do manifest what we think and that is a very positive experience. So, it is good to remember that we are part of a positive energy that lives in a Universe full of order and positive decisions. It is all a very natural, untethered process. The consciousness of the planet will always win and will always take care of itself. We have the same opportunity. And in all this positive energy is our very own Source and Supply. But we will never know about this if we do not allow ourselves to feel the Universe and everything in it. If we really want to have the formula to heal, we will become observers of nature, and listeners of the heart. In this formula there is no separation but we need both components to make this work for us. It promotes change without a struggle as the Universe does not struggle to survive and if there is something in it that has completed its cycle or journey, it will let go without struggle. An example is a falling star, a planet that dissipates, or any other phenomena that we are privileged to witness. There are adjustments made that we can use as a guidepost in our own lives.

With a positive Universe there is an opportunity to co-create. If our consciousness is in line we are easily co-creating for ourselves and others. We are active positive energy. Seen or not seen, we are making a difference without thought. Our thoughts become prayers of a positive nature once we have done our own healing, and we send these thoughts out among the vapors of the Universe. We are manifesting peace, love, help, healing or whatever we choose as our thoughts are no longer fleeting but have substance. Our unhealthy ego has transitioned into a state of awareness allowing the heart center to make all of our life decisions. Is that not the most positive action you could ever have? This is a positive life with the positive God of our understanding. Call this energy what you will and when you tap into it, and it changes your thinking to change everything in your life, you will have reached your personal Nirvana.

So are we really taking chances by being positive in a positive Universe? Until we as individuals learn this gift we will never know. We will be heard as not willing or willing. The Universe hears our thinking and even this becomes a positive. It is with deep love that we are reminded and suggested to in regards to being. It has been said to be careful what you pray for.

And with that in mind, it is as important to be careful what we think. What are you thinking? Take a moment right now and see what you are manifesting at this moment in your thoughts.

CAN WE HAVE A PERSONAL RELATIONSHIP WITH GOD?

In the quiet of a moment, we may ask to have a personal relationship with the God of our understanding. It does not need to be formal and there is no right or wrong way. No one is left out. The only ones left out are done by their thoughts and decisions. Healing addiction can last if we find our Spiritual Center and build a relationship on our own that works for us in the quiet stillness of our hearts. If we make the decision to remain separate and not available to this ONENESS Principle to have a relationship with the God of our understanding, it is seen as a positive decision until the next decision that will get us closer to a Higher Consciousness. We are not judged as we tarry along our way taking our time to have a Power greater than ourselves lead the way. We just stay with our same old lessons full of egotistical mind chatter. The ego is a master at helping us avoid or make wrong moves when it comes to our God connection.

We must surrender to what is the only dragon that can take down the ego and insure a loss of power. Once the dragon is wounded as it will never totally die, there will be a window of opportunity to hear things we have never heard until now. Our egos will not stay dormant for long…they get hungry to listen to the chatter and to convince us that they are the right one to follow. If there is anything dark that we need to learn to live with, it is the unhealthy ego. The ego will be the only thing that has the power to separate us from our truth, our Higher Self, and the Source and Supply that will give us peace. Addictions love the ego…because it says that it's okay, it's not an addiction, we can recover again, and it will not be so bad this time. Does this sound like a friend or an enemy? The choice we choose coming from the ego or the God of our understanding is what will attract the souls that mirror our journey and in the process will affect everyone in our life. Where we are going takes all of the souls with us.

LIFE AFTER THE TAMING OF THE EGO

It changes. It has to and automatically does. Without the ego running our lives, we are free to move into a new world, a new arena. We are free. At first it feels like a miracle but after a while of living with such understanding, and such peace, we may even realize that we didn't get a miracle, but we were the miracle. It almost feels magical. We are in perfect synchronicity with all that we do. And when we have a shift of thinking that no longer suits us, we have the understanding, the time put in, and the tools to be immediately on track. We are living in total light. By staying in the NOW and not future thinking or living our past as victims we are now ready to receive. We will keep getting Spiritual Riches and the Emotional Rags will be few. If we have an emotional rag, we will claim it and turn it over and keep moving on. This is exactly what happens to those who have made the decision to heal. The ego has no power left to stop our lights from shining through. How good it is to be able to recognize the wake-up call when we hear it.

BE YOUR OWN PHOENIX…REBIRTH

The legend of the Phoenix is one many of us know. This mythical bird lives for 3000 years, travels, engages with his destiny of lessons presented, and then grows old. At the end of his life he builds a nest of twigs and sticks and places himself in the middle while lighting a fire all around. The blaze in the sky can be seen for miles as the old bird is cremated and out to the ashes emerges a new Phoenix. A young and vibrant Phoenix to once again live out a lifetime of 3000 years. However in this new life he takes his new, strong and youthful self to flight with new lessons to learn, new lands to discover and new friends to meet.

The story of the Phoenix is what we are doing as we rebirth and let the old ideas die. We then move on with knowledge, wisdom and a new path. But there will be more to learn and to see. We will continue on a life-time, or rather life-times, of discovery. We are here to learn. And if addiction has taken us down to our knees with the Emotional Rags it comes with we can either be stubborn or thankful. Something had to get our attention. Something will always get everyone's attention. It is the way of the earthly visits that we keep making.

Gratitude for adversity can come to us if we are willing to let it open us up to the opportunity that we can now have. We have many lives and many lessons. However, lessons are why we are here. Lessons are what we went to school for. Lessons are good as they bring us more information that is filled with the knowledge we need to do our next right thing. We are amazing.

David Gregory

We are working our way through our lives to find a sacred contract that already lives within us. But with egoism, turmoil, addiction, and lack of commitment, we have been able to hear what we are here to do. When our lives get stopped, the Universe already knows we are ready even if we do not. The wake-up call takes what it takes to get there and when an emotional rag shows up, it is time to get serious.

As we start to show up to our life, not matter what age or economic income level we are at, we will notice our life is showing up to us. The questions will come. Are you ready to show up to the healing that needs to take place? Are you ready for your next step? Are you ready to let go?

This is always an independent personal, decision, and it is ultimately up to us. Our choices are always the game changers. The game of life has many faces. We have many faces. Who can we become today for the greater good of ourselves and all who know us?

By affirming our lives with our willingness to gather new information our immediate needs and dreams become our own reality. If we are wondering what is the new information that we need, we live with all the answers. Go to that still small voice once again. It is our only accurate and true voice that will intuitively give us the transformational information that we are seeking. Listen, learn and act on this timely life altering information with confidence. It is ours for the taking and will guide and pave the way to Spiritual Riches.

If we are living our life in the present moment, the information is in the present moment. Our job once again is to calm down and just listen. The most exciting revelation is that our NOW is building our great future in the present moment.

And as we build our future in our now, our dreams are realized to be more than frivolous daydreams. Our dreams are valid and they do show up if we learn how to show up to them.

102

SO YOU WANT TO WIN THE LOTTERY OR HAVE YOU?

Those of us who know that abundance is much more than the lottery are fortunate. And those who are still not aware of what total abundance means are still learning. For all of us, rich and poor, it becomes apparent at some point that money is not enough to bring us the peace and happiness we are seeking. If the Lottery is to be won and not squandered, it would be good to access all of our Riches right now. Let's take a look at what a real lottery looks like. We are our biggest investment. We are full of diversity, talent, and creativity. So by investing in ourselves we are investing in humanity. We have much to share and sharing unconditionally means that receiving comes naturally. Let's look around and see what is ours to have and share already. It most likely is the tip of the iceberg compared to what lies within us. Look to the Universe and affirm that it will provide more. Affirming that we are part of the Universe, one with the Universe, is a sure way to manifest anything that is of good intention. Enjoy the lottery you have already won. And do not squander thoughts on things you do not have yet. We need each other. There is always time to win more. Letting go of Emotional Rags and the Rags of addictions brings in a new dawn of change that is overflowing with the abundant Riches of the Universe.

LET'S START THINKING DIFFERENTLY RIGHT NOW

Let's look at new ways of thinking and get on with it. Manifesting our dreams is no dream that eludes us. Dreams can come true. Now is the time to start affirming our lives. Living in affirmations, not old worn out pity-pot thinking only brought us despair. For many a new way of thinking is a very old way of thinking. It came from the Universe long ago. Prior to the organized structure of religion and the tight hold on its members, there was a time before the world lost the practices of finding God in all things. Why would God create us without giving us the answer of all creation? Why are men of God judging us, telling us what we can and cannot do? Some of us need this structure. But there are many ready to embrace the power of God within. No punishing there. Instead just self-awareness, new and updated information and a GPS built-in to get us there. Mankind needed to evolve. Once we recognized that we had a direct connection, our thinking started to change. Churches today are still wonderful places to hear positive messages and meet good people. The churches of today are losing membership. Granted, some of them are becoming aware of this rally around new "old" thought. Denominations have to surrender to being open and affirming. Their thinking that was vengeful and judgmental is no longer working for many. It has come down to the final hour of change or lose membership. With membership goes the money that funds the institutions.

Churches of old were all about fundamental messages of fear, judgement, heaven and hell, depending on how good we were. Money was important and there was a push and a drive to fund the church with as much money as a parishioner could. It was a ticket to heaven that would miss the bus to Hell. Kings and Kingdoms joined with the church in expediting the process of getting as much money as possible. The churches got wise and turned this all around and became rich while controlling kings and kingdoms. This was the thinking then, but not now.

When changes started coming is when thinking people started asking questions. People started getting new information on their true connection to a loving God. When souls became ready to grow into a Higher Consciousness, a direct connection to the Universe and the personal relationship available to all people started appearing. People wanted a personal relationship with the God of their new understanding. The days of fear and judgement were gone. A new day had come with more truth and it continues to inundate the Universe. We are living in a New Age. We can heal ourselves and still have an understanding and connection to a Power greater than ourselves. The only difference being we have become ONE with our creator and the middle man is gone. This new thought on spirituality could be referred to as BLUE COLLAR SPIRITUALITY. We show up daily to our lives, we work and do our best daily and because we know the work ethic it takes, we feel and find the rewards of our new way of thinking. There is no need to buy a ticket to heaven as we have already bought a ticket for a heaven right where we stand. We have created our heaven in our now moments.

BLUE COLLAR SPIRITUALITY, simplistic in nature, creates an understanding of living in the now, finds us working with a determined due diligence, and finds us in a new way of letting go of our old ways of thinking on a regular basis. We have learned to show up and be available for what we need by being where we need to be in body or thought. If we go it alone, without a Higher Power, most of us practicing this way of living, have found that by trying too hard, there is more effort put into trying with a higher level of failure. But when showing up to our heart center on a daily basis there is no disease, no addiction, no negative thought that cannot be healed.

In learning any new principle, the only place to begin is at the beginning. But is this not true for everything we want to accomplish? By showing up with all engines running, a heart as porous as sponge, there is no way healing cannot take place. Humanity is in this world together to help, love, and heal each other by individual actions; every day we can take what we need and give what we need from each other leaving that which does not suit us at the time. How much more could we ever ask for from ourselves or others? We are experiencing not only the way to heal the wounds of our journey but the non-separation that has always existed. Up until a point in our lives we may have felt better or worse than others but with healing there is no separation. It is a "Yale to jail" experience. Oneness. No one is graded. There is no dunce hat or punishing corner in the room. Rather, there is support at every turn in every vapor of the Universe. We are connected and we will know this the moment we claim it.

A Personal Rags to Riches Story: I too had adversity growing up and it would become one of my biggest blessings.

My father's story at the end of his life I explained in an earlier chapter. This is a more personal story about my own challenged early life. There was no mistake that my Father was mentally challenged. Today, with more information on how to treat people with mental illness, he might have been able to be helped. However, it is important to know that he never took or wanted any kind of help.

He would have been diagnosed with multiple disorders, and when he finally was institutionalized all that really could be done for him in the late stages of many factors was sedate him with medications.

My mother, whom I dearly loved, was not available to me. As has been stated, she was a victim of a marriage that was abusive. Her main concern most of the time was managing my father's moods and protecting herself as well as she could under the adverse emotional draining circumstances. There was a great deal of fear in our household as we never knew what to expect from my mentally ill father. My mother, as well as the rest of the family, was on "high alert" at all times. We lived in fear of physical and verbal abuse. Looking back now, it feels as if I am telling a story, someone else's story, but this one really belongs to me. Terrorized by my father verbally, sexually, and physically, I remember sitting on the front steps of our home thinking about when I could leave. I was five years old. Looking at old pictures I see the pain in my brow at such a young age and the depression of feeling trapped.

My Emotional Rags affected my entire young life and continued to do so long after I was able to escape the jail that I had been born into. There were no hugs and kisses and kind words to be spread around. The dinner table was one of indigestion because of the constant verbal brutality. My mother tried to do her best I am sure. But she could not and would not be brave enough to stand up to this man who was destroying a family.

My brother, sister and I were not allowed to leave the property. There were no bikes. No after school activities and no Christmas or birthdays. There was only the words, "No you cannot," and "No, you won't," and "If you do...major consequences." The children at school, the neighbors, and even some of my Mother's relatives were not worthy of our time because they were not practicing Jehovah's Witnesses. Even though two Catholics flanked us on each side of our home, the people down the street and across the street were off limits to all of us. It was an isolating time and we were all trapped. My father took it upon himself to judge them because of their religion along with any other differences he could come up with. In the meantime in this small neighborhood where houses were very close, the neighbors were well aware of anger, fighting and yelling and four-letter words constantly coming from our house at all hours of the day and night until the crazy man behind the curtain was off to work.

The embarrassing accusations towards my mother could be heard. He had such a streak of darkness and meanness. He called her a whore, unworthy, stupid and anything else that came to his much-wounded, dark mind. He was gone during the day working but would show up at different times. Nights were very tough, especially when came home drunk and had my mother crying as he slammed and paced the floor pulling all of us children out of bed so we could watch his horror show. So we children were forced to cry along with her as the abuse continued into the wee hours of the morning.

These were our Emotional Rags that looked as if there would never be a way out of this horror story for any of us. These are what I call Emotional Rags. The Riches not even a thought at such a young age. But there was one Richness that happened everyday…my father left to go to work and was at least gone for a few hours. The energy was still muddled but there was a small reprieve. However, his work was changing, his emotional disease was getting worse and the story of this home and the inhabitants got worse, too. I had become deeply depressed. As I got older, I started getting more involved in the Kingdom Hall of Jehovah's Witnesses by doing the magazine placement and attending five meetings a week. This was my only escape out of the house.

At 16 years of age, I was questioning the religion I had grown up in because of its ridged beliefs. Now another set of Emotional Rags set in. So in my senior year of high school I moved out to my mother's tears and dismay. But oddly enough I knew she was secretly happy for me but sad for herself. I could no longer accept this religion that was feeling more like a cult and I definitely was not feeling the love of God but the fear of his wrath for all that was wrong with me. I had no relationship with God.

I was depressed and full of anxiety feeling that I was on the wrong track and the Witnesses would find me out. They did. They did because of an affair, short-lived that I had with a girl I worked with. It was my first experience with a woman. I was about 17. My mother found out because I had to tell my mother that the girl had told me she was pregnant. We had one encounter and I was unaware of the ways of the world to be snagged by a girl who wanted to get married. It was later found out to be untrue. However, I had been brought up with fear in regards to not coming forward with my immoral deeds and it was even worse if my mother was to know as she would be affected too if she did not let the committee of Jehovah's Witnesses know. I had to save my Mother. She knew and would not turn me in. So to save my Mother from dying in God's War, Armageddon, I had to confess to a committee at the Kingdom Hall where we worshiped and where I was no longer going.

I proceeded to let the elders know. Just one more emotional rag. I remember being totally shamed and embarrassed and red in the face from humiliation. I sat through a grueling meeting of many intimate questions about my one night affair. I was there to be judged. I was judged and then I was exonerated…with conditions. I did not like the conditions and never went back. I left a free young man with a few choice words under my breath. For some reason I was not dis-fellowshipped from that organization. The committee that judged me actually did dis-fellowship me because that is what I did on the way out the door. Today, as I look back, that was my first day of freedom from a life that was not serving me well. I admit I was mad at God and the Witnesses but I was free and if I had to die over freedom so be it. I finally began the journey back into letting the Rags go. There were many Emotional Rags that were ahead of me. To name a few: Depression, Low Self-Esteem, Dishonesty, Addiction, Sexual Orientation, The Journey Back to God, Judgments, Resentments, and the Learning How to Forgive…I am sure there are more.

I was at the start of a new life. The Phoenix in me sat on a pile of twigs and lit the fire so that I could be re-born with a chance to see the real world, a world that had all that I needed. I began. I am still here. I am going to keep going.

I promise you…I was born again but not saved. I had to save myself. Out of the Emotional Rags I personally found compassion, stopping myself before making judgments, release of resentments, and the gift of surrender and forgiveness. I share with others in knowing that these Riches are not for the few but for the many.

WE ARE BORN AGAIN TO FINISH SOMETHING IMPORTANT

We are born. For many of us this is not our first time around. We may not know this or maybe we have wondered why we are so comfortable in certain circumstances or why certain places or people we meet are so familiar. Without getting heady or intellectual about these experiences, it just is what it is and maybe we can open up to more possibilities as to why we are here and why we are with the people we are with in this lifetime.

Then again a new life from a past life can happen many times in this lifetime until we get to the point that we are giving away our sacred contract. What is our sacred contract? It can be as simple as giving away ourselves with transparency and authenticity as we show up to the arena of our life.

We all are here with unexplained gifts and talents that we can manifest without even thinking about it. These are our passions. They flow easily and are who we are.

If we look at nature around us and the way it works we can observe that there are indications of a reincarnation process. Dying is not an option. We may think it is. But there is nothing on this planet that dies. It may change form but it is not dead.

So I think we could agree that we are here to live. We may die to the life we have, but we are reborn to a new life with an opportunity for a new beginning in this life or the next. This helpful realization aids us in making sense of our lives. Fear at this point can be dismissed. Some know this naturally and others are here to evolve into the knowing that life is an eternity. It really makes no difference whether we buy into this thought or not. At the end of our lives, we will transition, and we will know for sure what we need to know for our next life. But while we are here…let's make life hum. Let's make life the passion that it is right now. Under all circumstances, if we are alive we are here to embrace this life and the lives of others with the way we give away our gifts.

As much as we may want to analyze past life experience, it really is of no use in the NOW of our lives in this instant. But there will be reminders of what we learned and what we still need to learn. There will be moments or flashbacks of some recognizable situation that we have been in or are in. Familiarity of knowing or feeling we have been somewhere or in the same situation happens to many of us and we have no explanation, yet it may feel odd and eerie but good. And that can be enough at the time to give us more clues as to our timeless presence in the Universe. But in the end, we are here to do our work, learn those lessons that give us more of who we are and then at the end of this life...move on.

This book is sharing with the reader that Emotional Rags are all part of this process. The adversity will bring prosperity and Spiritual Riches. Sometimes we need to be upset with what is so we can get to have what really is. There will be answers to every addiction, every relationship, and every challenge that we have. We are blessed with answers that live within and we can all get there. Take your turn. You will be amazed.

When we receive a nudge or sense of another lifetime, we may first feel fear. This is not very conventional, especially if we were brought up in one of the many fundamental religions of the world. But having an open mind and staying open to all possibilities will gives us an opportunity to at least explore all possibilities. The possibilities many times are the way we get what we need to move into a higher level of consciousness where more is revealed. If we are free of fear, this is where we would want to go anyway.

A new way of knowing can take us to a new place of living. By allowing ourselves to show up to some new thought, we become available to intuitive consideration of all of our options.

A practice, such as meditation and prayer or a quiet walk in the woods or staring deeply into the sky at the galaxies brings an awesome recognition of just knowing that we know.

CUSTOMIZE YOUR OWN JOURNEY

We all get to customize our journey and develop that special personal relationship with the Universe; that is the God of our very own understanding. Our Emotional Rags have the answers. It may seem odd that Emotional Rags can contain answers but without an emotional rag there would be no need for an answer.

Customizing our time and relationship with God usually has its beginning with the pain of an emotional rag. So showing up to new thoughts and giving your life a chance at having it all will surely prove to be a worthy investment in the time we give to knowing God. It is rather effortless or it can be very hard. Being that effortless is just recognizing that there is something bigger than ourselves to help us, guide us and love us makes our connection and relationship rather easy. But if we want to make our connection to God hard, we most likely are making everything in our life difficult. This is an emotional rag that really needs attention and quickly. There is help on the way if we are on the way to get it.

CHOICES, CHOICES, CHOICES…

Being born is one thing. Showing up is another. But as always, we have the choice. We had the choice in other lifetimes and we have the choice now. If we do not choose to grow and change, we will always get another chance. We are not judged but a loving God waits for us. The extravagant love that we are seeking is the extravagant love that lives within us. We are connected to it at all times, but the Rags get in our way. Once we intuitively know that we have a kind and loving God, our lives change because this new God is approachable. Thus our biggest emotional rag is gone. Once we know that the Universe works in our best interest, more and more Emotional Rags disappears. In a moment of sanity and simplicity, we realize that we have a chance to align with the planets and the stars and if we do…we are freely given the tools to complete what we have come to do. All in all it is recognition that there is no separation anywhere. Absolutely nowhere!

So the Emotional Rags are yet again saying, "You are living in the field of total opportunity and as you grow into your ONENESS you will be amazed at the steady progress that is made and before you are halfway through with your journey, major life changing shifts will occur. And as always with anything and everything we do, the best way to start is NOW." So are we addicted to starting and stopping as we are to falling in love or eating Twelve# of chocolate or drinking our guts out? Living in the NOW is our friend. We will get every answer we ever needed right now. The choice will remain ours. It has to be ours. Not our mother's, not our partner's, not our teachers', but ours. Once made, we will have all the support we need. It just happens and does so in a miraculous way. No explanation is needed for miracles. People who have recognized them can confirm this phenomenon.

It is good to take a glimpse at early life. Note the choices, the illusions, and the missed opportunities. But it will not help to dwell on early life. However, it is wise to see what has been stopping our making the best choices. So the needed answers are on what has been holding us back. What is it that keeps surfacing and affects how we live and how we think? What happened? What was going on? And what did it feel like? Are we still blaming our parents? Were our parents here to learn and grow too? Will we ever forgive them and let them have their own journey? Or are we going to let them stand in our way as we join their journey abandoning our own.

How did they do? And have we looked at their history to understand how and why they raised us in the way they did. Did our immediate family members get to grow and find their own way?

Whatever we felt that was challenging us in our early years were Emotional Rags our parent's dealt with too but were not successful in changing their story when we were growing up. What they are dealing with are most likely the same things their background challenged them with. The question can be posed in this way: What caused them to raise us in a way that left us with our current lessons?

And are we ready to put a halt to this ongoing lesson that keeps affecting generation after generation? How seldom we think of what they were learning. How often we want to blame them for what we think they did not learn. In doing so, our families take the heat of multi-generational Emotional Rags. Is this finally the opportunity to release what we think has been done to us? Are we willing to stop blaming and wish them well? What can we now do to grow and stop living in their energy field? Are we the ones called upon in this now moment to put a stop to this insanity? We are the ones who have the excellent opportunity to start healing the entire family by healing ourselves first.

What a moment of truth! What a Spiritual Richness that surrounds this new way of healing ourselves and our family. Yes, we do get this opportunity. But it becomes a choice in another now moment. Spiritual Riches are surely awaiting us if we make the right choice. So to have the Spiritual Riches, it will be worth the small amount of time to make a choice in a split second to change the way we have been thinking. Powerful life changes will occur on time and with ease. This is just another opportunity to surrender our old way of life.

SURRENDER TAKES WHAT IT TAKES

Many of us are very well trained at listening to an ego that has no intention of surrendering. When the ego is in full control of the soul, surrender is a weak and dirty word. That is why many of us have struggled so hard and so long to not give into the easier, softer way because we did not want to lose control. But in a challenging situation, haven't we already lost control when we have befriended the chatter of our ego instead of listening to the small still voice that will give us an answer that comes through our intuition? With the chatter of our monkey mind, we are still conjuring up whatever it takes, to handle what we are not able to handle with clarity. We are emotional, fearful and running rampant with crazy thoughts on how to fix the situation. We may even think we can fix a person and the situation and bring judgment and punishment to all that did not follow our direction.

Who could even hope to let go and surrender with all this self-sabotaging going on? We are the front page of our own news story and we are void of all the facts and all the help we need to bring this to a loving and sane closure. Addictively we hold onto our past decisions that never worked and we project our fear to ourselves and others if they do not listen to how to do what we want them to do. We need our God. We need Good Orderly Direction that can only come from a higher place, a place of sanity. We need to surrender and we finally will when what we want is so out of whack there is nothing else to do. But the toll it takes on ourselves and those around us creates a heaviness that is not necessary. Even at this point many cannot let go.

We may have wanted to let go, and some of us even put it in the editorial section of our front page news for a candid critique; it's our story and we would rather hold on to it than surrender to anything that could help us bring resolution. However, that fateful day arrives. We are totally exhausted with the way we do things. We tried to do things differently but we always took control not thinking to take a breath, ask a question and then let the answers come.

Addiction on so many levels will not allow us to have a Higher Power. It will not compete. It is our Higher Power and is running our lives. It is not willing to unleash us from the chains that bind us. Then comes a day when we are so exhausted trying to do all this change and surrender on our own, that we finally throw our hands and our mind in the air. We give up! We finally surrender to thinking that there has to be another way.

Surrendering this time we are too tired to keep taking our scattered chaotic Emotional Rags back. Maybe, just maybe, we have reached the breaking point of letting go and letting God. The ego is strong and may want to resuscitate us one more time. Is it fair to finally call this total insanity? Worn down and exhausted, there are still some of us who will try again. The ego will chatter away with a new plan and to our dismay, and even our surprise we will once again get the same results. This may be our last time to surrender and really stay with it. That extra oxygen tank that the ego seems to kick in as we are gasping for air and wanting to surrender is now pretty empty. It surely can take a lot to empty our tanks. In the end we will reach a time where the easier softer way is to catch ourselves when we are finding ourselves out of control to be in control. We are patiently waited for...and loved extravagantly when we arrive at the doorstep of a power greater than ourselves that wants us to have help we have all been promised. Many of us were taught that surrender is failure. Failure does actually not knowing when to surrender.

FAMILIES THAT HEAL TOGETHER DO SO...TO A POINT
In my family healing was not at the top of the list when I was growing up. Even later on in my young adult years, healing was not an option... yet. There were still lessons to learn which would bring us all to a point of willingness. Some were willing. Some were not. My mother seemed to be the first to pick herself up, dust herself off and proclaim a new life after she divorced my father. She had a very deep survival technique that she used from her own childhood.

There were three children born to this family of many lessons and early on my brother at the young age of 18 was killed in an automobile accident. My mother, too, had a history of addiction and abuse from her family of birth. But it was her deep commitment to herself that finally kicked in and saved her life. She made a great deal of progress in the second half of her life. She began the process of healing the wounds that needed healing and it became an opportunity for all of us to heal. We had watched her own surrender and the way she picked herself up and started living her life once again. It became a total rebirth for her and she was already in her mid-forties. In the Now of all our lives, the Emotional Past had happened. There was no denying it or sweeping under the carpet.

When we heal from addictive relationships, or mind altering substances, there comes a time when we either surrender or lose the rest of our lives to despair. But in her case, healing became the hallmark of her recovery by showing up and continuing to let go of the past. I feel blessed with her love and life and the way she showed us the way without even realizing what a great example she had given us to follow. She too had a hard early life. But with the God of her understanding and the willingness to change a life of lessons that she was done with, the rest of her life was full of Spiritual Riches.

SOME WILL…SOME WON'T…HEAL

Many experiences in our lives are filled with hurt, fear, and abandonment. But coming to realize that our own Emotional Rags of hurt, fear, and abandonment are the gateway to opportunity can become a new and different way of thinking. Just because our family has gotten us off to a rough start, does not mean we cannot heal and get on with it.

Opportunity comes to many of us in many strange unintended ways. My Mother and her Emotional Rags which needed healing were right in front of her as they are in all us. I championed her efforts with love and support and in the end she championed mine the same way. She did the best she could at the time and all the time right up until she surrendered. Most of us do. Years later we would have a conversation in which she revealed to me that she wished she could have been better, done better. I assured her the best I could that she had done a great job with her children and her two marriages. She knew how to love and we cannot go wrong if we know what deep love does, and how it feels, and what it gives to others. She also learned how to surrender and how to express herself authentically.

IT TAKES WHAT IT TAKES

How often many of us feel that we are not enough; that we have not done enough and wish we could have done things differently. But until we walk through a situation, mistakes and all, we will never know what the opportunity is and how to change. But the truth for me is that as for my mother and for all of us, it just takes what it takes to get us where we need to go. Isn't that the reality of what surrender really looks like? Is it not plausible that some of us become addictive so we can be stopped at some point to learn? What else would have or could have worked? We will never know but one thing for sure we are all right on time.

So we may ask ourselves, in the letting go process, what is the right way and what is the wrong way? Can I do it? More honestly, will I do it?

Are we not better and more compassionate because of all these Emotional Rags?

And my experience and conclusion to this question is, yes, we are, once we have walked our talk and surrendered to the Emotional Rags, we will not know the Riches that are waiting for us. It is the yin and the yang of life. It is our black and white with shades of grey. We do survive the process as uncomfortable as it may be. We can finally let go. We can let God. We can be free.

When all is said and done, we come to understand that it is easier to heal than not to heal. The experience of healing our Rags promotes a quick turn-around on any new ones that may try to infiltrate our life. Oh, well. We are ready. We have learned. We will know that Emotional Rags are the road to Spiritual Riches and we know that road. We have taken that trip more than once.

Patience will come to be a very important part of our journey. It helps to remind ourselves that the Universe is always on time. We live. We learn. We grow. We move on. My mother moved on at 75 and is now in the bliss of what she would call her heaven. She visits me regularly. She is supportive and has been with me in many lifetimes. When our own dust clears, we are so much clearer with what we intuitively know. I have not lost her and I will be so happy to be with her for an extended length of time before I return to planet Earth. We are so connected and have always been. That to me is Rich.

LET'S STOP OUR RED WINING, A PERSONAL ACCOUNT

This chapter happens to be more on the Emotional Rags of addiction, but for those of us who have used any substance, including food, sex, or gambling to escape ourselves will understand the Emotional Rags of this continued revelation of the consequences of addiction.

Personally speaking, red wine was my drug of choice and so was white and so was vodka and so was beer. I think I have made my point... There was not a winery big enough to service my needs or so I thought. White wine, red wine was also my "whine" of choice and Mr. Fix It. And martinis with double olives, straight up, in a classy crystal martini glass. Silently I would whine and be fixing everything but me. "No ice" was a drug I used when

I wanted to feel like a classy guy who knew how to medicate with style. I used to not want any drink served on the rocks as, "It just gets in my way!" And yet I still called myself a social drinker. I must admit that at the time, alcohol was the medication that kept me from meditating. It was my unhealthy friend. It soothed my troubled soul and kept my ego active with justification. I was secretly troubled with my own Emotional Rags. What was there to address or admit when my best buddy understood? Alcohol was my buddy and definitely my drug of choice. I always got hit back hard but that was just how my buddy was. My buddy was abusive but I was used to abuse.

I never complained or whined outwardly but I always took my buzz to the finish line and blocked out an entire lifetime in three to six hours or passed out. My whining was always painfully living inside me darkening my soul. I was hiding with addiction as my screen.

When I came to in the morning, my Emotional Rags were still blocked out as my hangovers were always brutal and of course got worse the longer time span that I indulged. Underneath the hangovers and the alcohol were a million or so Emotional Rags that my ego relentlessly would not let me forget. And in any kind of hurting and painful sober state, I would be reminded. I sometimes got a short reprieve in the mornings only because I had to manage the hangover.

And then my chattering monkey mind would start the chatter and remind me of the years gone and future fears of Emotional Rags that were nagging in my head. They would not let up. They would not go away or maybe I would not let them go away. But of course I had the antidote, I had the fix. I would start the process of taking the Emotional Rags away with the medication that was legal and worked for me. Wine, beer, martinis, straight vodka....whatever silenced the chatter the quickest and then I could be someone else that never had problems or issues. Right? Wrong! I thought this was normal.

THE NECTAR OF THE GODS WAS KILLING ME

The nectar of the Gods worked until it didn't work. That day came as the disease of alcoholism has a beginning, middle and an end. When the time came and I could no longer function, I was a 24/7 drinker, I knew my time was up. My Emotional Rags could no longer be shut out with my drinking. My emotions were harder to hide and in the end there was no way to do so. The jig was up. I was caught in my own mess. Only this was one of the biggest Emotional Rag messes I had ever had to address. It was full of layers and layers of Emotional Rags that had been swept away and hidden. It was the tip of my iceberg. I had so many Emotional Rags stuffed inside me that once the alcohol was gone, I was exposed. Yes, totally exposed… to this thing called life. My life, the real life I had lived and was living. I felt naked and vulnerable as never before. I remember being so afraid and so fearful. It made me want to run back to the dis-ease that no longer worked. I would heal or die and I knew it.

I WAS DYING FOR A DRINK…AND GOT CLOSE!

Oh my God…it was time to do one of two things. Either keep drinking and die young or stop drinking and die old. Dying young meant to me taking with me these Rags of emotion, drama, and addiction to another life. Oh, how I did not want to do this again. That did not feel like a good option. In all conscious sanity which was very little at that time, I could not imagine having to do this lifetime again.

I had been somewhat aware of my spiritual connection for a long time. God was not new to me. Yet I had not actually accessed the help I needed. Pride stood in my way. I kept hearing that I had work to do. I put off the work with every drink I drank and every hangover I recovered from with a drink. I never realized how much work it would take to dispel my demons. I was full of shame and remorse and felt very uneasy about talking to God about what the Divine already knew.

Today, many years later, my shame is gone. My big Emotional Rags that felt like I could never conquer are gone. I still have Emotional Rags to work on but the big work is over. I am on a Self-High Watch program of keeping an open eye and ear on whatever wants to take my peace away. I am on High Watch when it comes to fear, judgments, and resentments I have learned from my past but no longer live there. It is gone and I admit that it is gone. Until I came to know the truth about who I was and why I was doing what I was doing to hide my life, I could not heal. It took every drink, every hangover, and ever negative experience I had to bring me to my knees. This is where I came to a point of willingness. But for me it took hitting rock bottom before I was ready to be willing.

I know I am not alone when it comes to any kind of addiction as I am once more sobered up and I took a look at the way I lived and where my focus was. Everyone will get the nudge to heal at one time or another. Almost everyone, if they are ready to listen, will not be able to ignore the nudge of changes that need to be made. Some of us have it harder when it comes to change and we need a harder lesson.

The nudges are not just from alcohol when it comes to addictive behavior. It can be anything from alcohol to any other addiction such as gambling, working out, a relationship, food…the list goes on and on. But when the wake-up comes with either a soft nudge or one that hits us over the head, we are then able to at least have the chance to make a change in our lives. It takes help for us meet ourselves in the light of our moment of truth. This is why I choose to share my story in an effort to relate and help others by giving them the hope that was given me. I hid addiction. I am not going to hide healing as if I never needed them. My ego has long been checked at the front door of my soul.

LET'S LOOK THE OTHER WAY…
LET'S PRETEND, LET'S NOT!
It is my observation that it becomes second nature to look the other way and not accept the help to survive terrible emotional traumas and dramas. Hiding can come more natural. Why should anyone ever really know me? Why would I let them?

My family had the dis-ease of hiding alcoholism and I was a perfect candidate to use this substance and this method of living to hide for 40 years of my life.

When asked, I tell people that when I was in my emotional rag, I needed every drop until I dropped. It kept me sedated and shut down until I was ready to heal. Yes, I am one of those who wished I had gotten the memo sooner, but that was not me. I had to face my own music and was forced onto my own stage front and center and the world was my audience. I felt totally unsure of myself. I had regressed to that openly depressed little boy who was waiting to escape his family of birth and the home that was the closest experience to a living Hell I had ever known.

What was I to do? What was I going to do and how was I going to be able to even show up? I had to put one foot in front of the other and no matter what… just start one day at a time to show up.

My days of showing up were slowly happening. My feet were dragging for a long time. It felt as if I was having a huge growth spurt and my arms and legs did not know where to go. I was so out of sync and everything and everybody looked foreign to me. Oh well.

To heal is to stand emotionally naked and start asking for help. AA was my first stop, and it helped for years. I definitely have AA on the to-do list for anyone addicted to drugs and alcohol. Bill Wilson's Twelve Step Program gave me my life back. However, if I had not been willing to participate in the Spiritual part of this program, I doubt that I would be who I am today. I might be sober but I am not convinced that I would be happy.

Addiction to alcohol is very common because it is legal. When there is a substance that, when used properly, can enhance us socially, we rarely need to look at the abuse that can happen. I was not a social drinker. I never liked alcohol but I liked the affect it gave me. I smoothed out. I finally relaxed my chattering mind. I became an illusion of who I may have really been. But I had a long way to go sober to get to the roots of my soul.

It is not the quick fix most of us hope for. It is a temporary fix and the reason we use is for most of us at the time we are sorting through our fears, emotions, and lack of self-esteem, it is helpful. We got a temporary reprieve. In the end, at the bewitching hour, this kind of addiction is no longer working. We realize, as we try to sober up, that we have added another layer of an emotional rag that will take some real willingness and concentration to heal. If we ever want to have a real life we have to address the addictive one first and then be willing to go after the layers of pain that we used our addiction for.

All in all, the family disease has little to do with addiction at first. It is the first drink one takes that can catch our attention. Our body absorbs the feeling quickly and in the months and years to come, we will need more and more to hold that feeling that we think is setting us free. Little do we know, at the outset, that our addictions are actually confining us to a life of living without the benefits of knowing who we really are. It will take everything away from us starting with material possessions, homes, jobs, and family and at the very end we will lose our sanity. This is not a drug that will cure us but instead, it will attempt to first kill our insides and then take everything else that is ours including a healthy body and leave it for dead. Even without physically dying, at the end of this disease that stopped working, we would rather be dead.

If we are fortunate to realize that we have a gene that runs in families and is sitting within us to destroy our lives as opposed to helping us, we have a chance. And if we slip and slide in and out of addiction this disease is so cunning that it will immediately pick up where it left off. Only the next time it comes at us with a vengeance. It wants our body, mind and soul. It gets harder and harder to sober up when we keep picking up.

A CURSE SELF-INDUCED WITH A REMEDY

It is a curse that is self-induced, for whatever reason we think we need it, but there is a way out if we are willing. Anyone of us has the capability, the strength and the help to conquer this insidious disease. First we have to be willing, then we will have to commit to showing up and the way we can do this is with the relationship that we will need to build with something bigger and stronger than ourselves to beat this addiction. We may stay sober for a while but without the help of others and our Higher Power the chances are slim that we can maintain a stable and successfully life-long sobriety. To become drama free from our addiction, we need to engage in the drama until it is released for good. There are those in the rooms of

AA that have already gone through what we are attempting to do. It has been recommended that we get a sponsor whom we can trust and work the Twelve steps. This is a willingness step for us. But the willingness to change the way we think so we can change our life is crucial to our recovery. It cannot and will not happen without help.

With the brain freeing up and clarity of where we are in the moment, we have some opportunities to start the most important part of the rest of our lives: listening...really listening. We all have been given the gift of having everything we need and this information lives in the still small voice of the God of our understanding. This Higher Conscious Source and Supply has always been there for us. We, on the other hand, are here to learn the way to have this gift start to help us manifest who we really are. We have had the life of illusion and discontent and know we have the opportunity to get tuned in for the remaining time we are here.

Many people first addressing addiction, never think to go to a Source bigger than themselves. They have always been the big one in their own lives struggling to make things work their way. But when we hit our knees, when all the stops are out, when body, mind, and spirit call it quits, we are all usually ready to do anything to get the help we need. It takes what it takes and this is what it took for many of us. So the question arises... what's next? How do I make contact? How can I keep the contact going? To answer these three vital questions please let me show you what worked for me and others:

1. We need to do the next right thing all the time.

2. Making contact with a God of our understanding is merely a thought away. Those who are struggling with "God," may need to pick their own Higher Power. Or at least recognize that we have something bigger than ourselves to help us.

3. To keep the contact going is first of all to know that the contact has never left you. The contact has and will always be there for the asking. We are the ones who have the responsibility to show up to our Source and Supply.

ASKING IS RECEIVING

We have to ask in our own way in the silence of a thought, prayer, meditation, or even screaming out in the middle of the night. If that is the way we approach our Higher Power so be it. We will be heard. Affirming that we have this beautiful energy that is the Universe and lives within us is the next important thought to have. If doubt occurs, doubt occurs. It is all part of learning to trust. That is why after years of addiction we take baby steps to re-enter our lives. We need a beginning and we will find that we are the beginning. Once we are ready, the teachers appear the God of our understanding is made known.

By acknowledging that we are finally aware, means the healing process has already started. We are on the cliff of dumping a lifetime of Emotional Rags. Yes, finally knowing in itself is an affirmation of being ready and will attract a life changing experience.

Because of our willingness to begin we have already accessed enlightenment. It is in front of us to teach us. It will come through on many levels whether it is with others or in the quiet time of a personal meditation. There is work to do but who does not have a need of putting time when it is the beginning of experiencing a final goal and gift in the end? We all have to take a long walk in the woods with any kind of addiction that took us out of our now. Now we are walking out and it will take time to leave the deep forest we penetrated. But the open fields are there waiting for us. And the walk we are taking out of the woods is one that allows us to leave much of what no longer works for us on the path we know we are leaving behind.

THE FEELINGS START COMING…
GO AWAY! THEY WOULD NOT

It was a hard time at the beginning to sober up. All the feelings I had felt were surfacing. There was so many and they kept repeating in the chatter of my unhealthy ego. The very feeling I was facing was the reason I started to drink in the first place.

I was detoxing, feeling quite unsteady, and faced with years of feelings that dated all the way back to my early childhood. And it was not only the recent sobering up predicament I was in; it seemed to be everything plus a little bit more.

In my experience, I had to face another emotional rag. I needed to come out of the closet of being gay. I was in and out my whole life because I played the game of not have total acceptance of myself. My acceptance of my being gay was staring me in the face. The hiding was over. My feelings were on the outer layer of my skin. I felt so totally exposed. It was frightening. There was nowhere to go and nowhere to hide anymore. My spending 28 days in Lakeside Treatment Center in the state of Washington had been rather safe. Everybody was there for the same reason. It was like being in a gay bar for the first time and realizing that other people were like you too.

SOBER OR DRY...THERE IS A DIFFERENCE

After 28 days without alcohol I was sober when I left. I would rather say I was dry. Sober is free of alcohol where dry is not drinking but wanting to. My thoughts were not about sobriety. I wanted to drink but had all these flashes in my head of what I had learned about alcoholism: why I drank, what the disease was all about, that I was in late stage with a damaged liver, and the shakes that made me start my morning drinking to get rid of the hangovers. Leaving the treatment center was scary. I was raw. Returning to work was scary. Living at all was scary. I was so out of a normal element for me. My life was now AA meetings, AA meetings, and more meetings. I went until about three months of feeling so out of sync and so lost that I asked a sober person in the program of AA why I felt so badly and she said to me that it just gets worse. She had five years in the program and had been on the staff when I checked into Lakeside Treatment Center. Her answer took me over the edge...Worse was not what I needed to hear but it gave me the permission I was looking for... to drink. If after five years she was still feeling miserable like me, then I was not going to stay sober one more minute. A healthy person in recovery would tell someone that it only gets better. Because it does for those who are willing to show up on a daily basis and use the tools of the program of AA.

I drank. I drank until I was sedated, and then until I was drunk and passed out. But this time I had too much information and it was the worst hangover I had ever had combined with the guilt of failure. I now had to continue to drink or start over. I started over. I got back on the shaky track and suffered through more meetings, discomfort, and doubt that I could ever make it.

LOOKING FOR AN EXCUSE MEANS WE ARE NOT DONE

There are many reasons for a recovering addictive person to pick up the drug that works for them: the loss of a job, the start of a new job, the loss of a relationship, the starting up of a new relationship, a hang nail or a bad haircut. You name it and that can sound like a great reason to check out with an addictive solution. Here is my story of what it took.

I got a job offer in Sarasota, Florida. I went to a company for a friend and co-worker of mine from a previous job. I arrived and had been sober for a few months and was beginning to feel better and confident again. Confidence can be a danger sign. I was hired as the Marketing Director for a new construction company. I would be entertaining prospective clients and be in charge of securing new work.

My mind had a million reasons as to why I would need to pick up a drink. I became very important in my own mind. I would be socializing with new perspective clients. We would be out for lunches and dinners and I would need to have a drink or two just to be social and make sure that they were comfortable with me when they ordered a drink. It sounded so reasonable. So I showed up to my new job and was sure that the alcoholism that I had learned about and worked on was now gone. I was fine. So I socially started to drink...for about one day. My still soggy brain, with very little time in recovery, informed me along with my low self-esteem that this was the way to go if I was to be successful finding new business. My chattering ego had stepped in again and I could not hear the small still voice of reason that lived within. But of course the truth was I did not want to listen to reason on this topic.

The job went *okay* until once again…my fragile self got some indication that my sexuality had come up and I had been out-ed. Fear set in and drinking increased with not enough alcohol to silence that chattering monkey mind that had totally taken over. I thought that I had heard the owner say something on a telephone referring to me. He had a private office. The door was open and I thought that I was privy to the conversation. Did I? Did I imagine it? Why would it matter? I was doing a good job. But that no longer mattered. I was obsessed with the thought that he and others might think that I was a "Gay Man."

I don't know if that happened to this day. I drank alcoholically from that time on but I was really already well-vested in the disease I had tried to recover from. I reacted and did some out of character things among one in particular. I wrote a letter of resignation calling him on something I was not even sure of. I copied his wife and a few thousand others…. Oh my God, what had I done. Since that fateful day many years ago, I have had the pleasure of making my amends to this wonderful man and his lovely wife. They were so good to me about the whole crazy thing I did with my bottle by my side. We remain close friends and little did I know that his oldest son was gay and was never abandoned but loved unconditionally by the entire family. My shame has healed because of their love. I went back to my program for healing. Was I done? After one year of sobriety and making some major progress I still was not done with this disease.

MY EXTENDED FAMILY ONCE AGAIN SAVES ME FROM ME

I was back at it. The job went badly; I was unable to stay sober because even with some time in I had limited coping skills. My back went out and I downed too many pain pills with alcohol and proceeded to have a nervous breakdown. This was the hardest bottom I had ever hit so far.

My best friend's mother and dad rescued me again along with my best friend Mary. It all happened miraculously as they swooped in, gathered me up and got me back home, which was their home.

They loved me unconditionally and always believed in me and assured me that under all circumstances, I would always land on my feet. They could never wrap the idea around their brains that I was an active alcoholic. It was too hard for them to admit. They were sure that once I had some rest and time with them I would be okay. Part of that was true. But I needed to once again find my way into the rooms of AA.

Most importantly, I was blessed with another very special friend who walked though my ups and downs for about four years. We spoke on the phone every day for years.

Her name is Judy and she to this day is one of my most loved and devoted friends. I had lived with Judy early on in my sobriety and she was truly a gift from God. Judy for some reason was able to get through to me spiritually. She was a very important part of my life and still is years later. She is a very special lady who came into my life and championed my efforts.

Her life in a wheelchair from polio at a young age never stopped her progress to becoming a business owner, driving a van, and even going sailing with her boyfriend. Judy is an inspiration as to what can be done with a handicap. I definitely had one. She would always have one and I was the one that could leave mine behind.

She also was involved in the community and we both sat on a Board for Attitudinal Healing. This was a wonderful program started by Gerald Jampolsky which met weekly to teach the formulas to heal attitude to change lives. She introduced me to a more in-depth understanding in my spiritual growth and was a great support as I returned to college. She truly loved me and supported my efforts. She was well aware of alcoholism as her father had also been an alcoholic. She had to be an Angel. I am so blessed. I lived with her while attending college until I returned to work in LA.

AFTER ONE YEAR...I GOT THE CURE OR DID I?
I had been on a vacation with Judy and felt spiritually fit and was ready to have a drink. Is that not insane? I remember my prayer. God, if I ever have a problem with alcohol again, I will return to AA. I felt cured. Little did I realize that being cured was not drinking. Drinking was being sick again with this insidious dis-ease.

I had my drinks and began monitoring my intake of alcohol. People who are social drinkers do not need to monitor their usage. That never occurred to me at the time. I was just done with AA and grateful for my time there as that had been my safe place to get well. But in my still sick head, I was sure I no longer needed those meetings or those people.

GOD SENDS ME ON MY WAY…MY FRIEND IS SAVED!

The job offer came at a perfect time as it was time for me to leave Judy and learn my next lesson. The company offered me a six figure income. I was on my way after a year and a half of college and no drinking until now. I was feeling well and fit. I had learned a great deal but time would prove that I had not learned enough…yet. I felt so good that I became willing to put my life on the line again and risk it all because of the love of a liquid substance that could take my life away.

Eventually in LA the same thing happened to me that happened before. I became a daily drinker, including mornings. I could hardly wait for the weekends and I was always hurrying home from my job to have my drinks. My stress levels were up and yet somehow by the grace of God I was able to do a good job for the company I worked for. I was monitoring everything. I did a good job and maintained but I know I was being protected but not for long as the bigger lesson was yet to come.

I was on my way to Louisiana for another contract job. I worked from home. How convenient for an alcoholic. I did not work very much that year. Oh I got by, but barely. And then the job was finished and off I was again to another part of the country for another project job. The journey continued but now it had to stop. I was a mess. My next job took me to Richmond, Virginia for a management job that I was not prepared to handle. Because of my drinking I ended up having a nervous breakdown after mixing pills and booze. I almost died.

Did I stop drinking? No. I could not handle the state of Emotional Rags I was in to come off all the alcohol and pills that made me unable to do anything.

So I managed the disease the best I could under the circumstance of having a breakdown but I needed another rescue. I got it from home, moved back again and tried my best to sober up. But I could not get there. I was not able to stop...even with meetings...even with a sponsor. My disease was holding me hostage. I finally got another job offer in New Jersey. I showed up in a very unstable state of mind, went immediately to a bar, and ordered a glass of white wine.

For the first time in my life I was unable to drink it. Something had happened. I was getting an intervention from something bigger than myself. The Universe and the God of my understanding had stepped in. I was finally at a full surrender, unable to drink, and in need of all the help I could get. I was at the mercy of the Universe and was ready to do anything to stop my drinking. And this is what it takes to stop addiction. I was willing to do anything to stop doing what I was doing because I kept getting what I was getting because of it.

After a few days, I showed up to an AA meeting. I felt totally withdrawn and guilty for not being able to stay sober. I met a man called Joe, who was older, and who actually knew the founder of Alcoholics Anonymous (AA), Bill W. We talked, I shared my story, and he felt my guilt. He said just one statement to me, "David, you are still loved. You are a good person. Pick up where you left off, and get on with it." That was 16 years ago. He was the biggest piece of gold I have ever witnessed; a true example of Spiritual Riches. He told me something that I desperately needed to hear. And I heard him which in itself is amazing under the circumstances. I thank God for Joe. Spirit gave me a nudge through Joe. I listened to Joe, got involved by taking on service work. I stayed sober, the disease was lifted. I had truly surrendered and by God's Grace I have had an incredible sober life since then. I do know what it takes to surrender. It was the hardest thing I ever have done.

IT TAKES WHAT IT TAKES

For some reason...my ego had to go through all that it did to get my attention. I was full of chatter. When I look back, I know that everything that had happened to me at its hardest I needed to happen. My ego had been in full control and it did not want me to surrender. It took a deep spiritual surrender that is hard to explain but something that is deeply felt.

The fear, the doubt, the depression all played an important role in my waking up. Thank God, I did not stop trying to become sober. The God of my understanding, the God that we all have a personal relationship with, if we want it, was waiting for my commitment and my surrender. I had done this once before but I got "well" or so my over eager ego persuaded me to think. Thank God for letting me know that the Rags of adversity were the bridge of opportunity to a life I could only imagine. Without the pain…I would have never sobered up. Without the help of others my chances of recovery would have been nil. Without the God of my understanding in my life, sobriety would have been impossible.

The Riches I finally realized could happen and be not only recognized, but a reality even while being in the despair of Emotional Rags.

It takes what it takes for all of us no matter what we are changing when it comes to addictions. So what did all this change and enlightenment do for me?

I stopped my judging everything and everybody because of my own insecurities when it came to changing my thinking. Resentments were tamed with compassion. However the biggest change really seeing life and who we are, is losing a constant fear of just about everything. With the fear I had I lost my freedom to be. To be the person I really was. It became clear that the judging and resenting along with comparing was all linked to my deep rooted fear. I had just won my own lottery.

IT WAS TIME TO SLAY THE DRAGON

Now when the dragon of fear appears, I now have tools to help me slay this dragon that has been following me around all of my life. But without that dragon hot on my heels, I would never have arrived today with a deep understanding of addiction and so many other things. Once we slay our dragon, we will be able to move into our Sacred Contract. That contract is the one we do best in this human form on the planet earth. There are many of us who are still looking for our purpose and without realizing it the ones looking are many times already in their contract or purpose. I say contracts because it has been revealed to me that we have many sacred contracts depending on where we are with our Spiritual Journey.

FAMILIES THAT RAG TOGETHER DO NOT HEAL

Most all of us have a certain love for our families. Therefore, we want to fix what we don't like. We think this is the way we can really love them, and they, in turn, will really love and understand us. We actually sometimes think we can change our families to be more acceptable of our own personal needs. If our family members would only listen to us! There is one thing we can be assured of and that is - they are not going to change for us.

SO WHO IS GOING TO CHANGE?

Many times after several jump starts to change others, there comes this clear message that, "Oh my God, it is me that has to change!" And, as we get healthier, we begin to realize that our job is for us to change and that changing others is not only out of the question but it never worked before and it is not going to work now.

Everyone is entitled to his or her own journey. We are not fixers, but we are also not enablers. Why prolong our own journeys or the journeys of others by convincing them to change when all we get out of it is a temporary fix, if that.

Truthfully, in order to grow out of Emotional Rags; we need to address our own journeys. That is our direct path to enlightenment. We cannot even begin to heal until we have finally been enlightened. We may stumble on new information that will help us or we will get the nudge of a lifetime that we are finally hearing.

"Well you know…" can be a very scary start to a sentence. It is the start to someone ready to tell us what to do, what we should think, and why he or she knows the answers to our problems.

You "should" is also an ambush put on someone. If we are to face our own challenges, the "should" as nice as they are put to us, just do not work. Who is unable to listen, as we answer, face our challenges and heal ourselves? People just do not hear us, and we definitely do not hear them. *No one is listening to the ranting or ego of another. No one wants that kind of advice. And in the end with or without our crafty, well-executed advice nothing changes in another until we address the changes needed under the premise that we are all in this for the greater good of all.*

While we are living in our own Emotional Rags, we cannot fix anyone. And, once we have found our way, we find there is no need to fix anyone. We let go of one more Emotional Rag and find that we are becoming wiser, and more connected, along with being an empathetic and caring listener. Some of us never were or, may I say, "I never was..." There was always for me, 'way too much chatter in daily life to be able to listen carefully. I personally had not learned how to shut down and get quiet as I prepared for the answers I needed. When it comes to fixing ourselves, it takes a universe full of guides, angels, and a God of our understanding, who patiently places "listening champions" in our paths. Their help is all about support. That is what I finally learned. Call them what you want but there is a higher dimension of help that gets us to where we need to go to learn what we finally learn.

OTHER PEOPLE FULL OF EGOIC CHATTER CANNOT HELP US

One of the most obvious signs of someone who is not ready to be our champion, is someone who is struggling to quiet their own mind. This person also has not found his or her way to connect with a higher consciousness.

As we even begin to learn how to live a ONENESS principle, we begin the journey of healing and understanding that all of us are on the same journey at one level or another. The ego, if allowed by us, would like to have its hold on us. We all get to a point in time when we realize that the unhealthy ego does not have the answers. But, most importantly, we finally understand that no one's egoism help is going to "cure" us.

Our heart center has the answer. And anyone telling us what we should do only complicates our own healing processes.

FAMILY AND FRIENDS TEND TO SPY ON US

Close friends and family can be busy monitoring our lives, comparing our journeys with theirs, and are ready to jump in with all the answers… When this happens, they are out of their own journey and into ours abandoning the attention needed to their own journeys, which most times can be quite disheveled as they watch to try and fix ours. This, many times, unintentional advice that has all the answers is more directed at what they are trying to change with an existing situation like or unlike the one we are in. In other words, their intent interest in our lives is more about their own lives. At any point any of us can find that we are pulling out of our own lessons to fix another so we can ignore or sidestep the work we need to be doing.

WE ARE ALL GETTING THE SAME LESSON AT SOME POINT

Anyone trying to tell another unhealthy person what they need to be doing and how to change their life turns into a major derailment that we too can easily be sucked into. Healthy relationships are born and maintained by example, listening, and a suggestion relating back to our own lives.

When we butt into another's journey asked or not, anger, fear, and resentment are the results and we have only created a train wreck that may be very hard to set right.

We cannot discount the fact that we absolutely need our champions for support. The safest and most helpful souls in our lives are the ones who listen, support, and make suggestions based on their own experiences. If we have these gifts in our lives, we are able to make headway in our own personal growth. We are also able to learn, by example, what really works in healthy supportive relationships.

These helpful champions, who share by listening and supporting us in our Emotional Rags, are the true gift we need when we are in a state of confusion and change. At the end of our listening period, a healthy listener emerges healthy and supportive of our best intentions. A good listener already knows that we know. They will do their best to ask the questions that nudge us into our own answers. He or she then let's go and lets God.

They have chosen to love us, until we can love ourselves, by allowing the answers we need to come through from our Source and Supply, the God of our understanding. *What a gift!* They are our earthly angels standing by until we see our own wings sprout.

OUR FAMILIES CAN BE OUR GREATEST TEACHERS

We are connected to our birth families for good reason. Our goal with family Rags is to heal the Emotional Rags that come with them, so that we can move on to our own next level of service to the universe. When we challenge the family Rags that have kept us down we are available for the Spiritual Riches to appear.

Birth families are sometimes the hardest lessons we have. They give us the most opportunity to grow because of the deep connection they hold. Even with all the love that is there seen or unseen, families have dynamics that can challenge our peace and happiness let alone our thought processes. Common statements like, "I will never be like my mother," "My father's behavior with verbal abuse, alcoholic drinking and indiscretions against my mother will never be something I would do to my family." "I would never…" is a dangerous statement in a family setting with dynamics that are part of the family unit. We are in the family of birth to mirror what needs to be seen in ourselves and to be there for the rest of the family with unconditional love. If we are not learning from the family, we become the family that has not healed. If we are learning from our family of birth, we will not need to maintain the behaviors, whether they have or not. We will move on. We will understand more fully why the behaviors are there and our compassionate side will rule out anger, judgment and resentments. We will find that we are actually forgiving what we thought they did to us. In the Rags of a family dynamic, they are actually teaching us what we need to know for this lifetime. The Riches we will receive are many. Once we let go of old family behaviors or how they have affected us we are truly free. All family members are not going to heal this time around. Some will and some will not. But this cannot be our focus, or our job to do. We are going to need all of our attention to embrace our own healing when it comes to our family of birth.

135

OUR HEALING DOES NOT ALWAYS GO UNNOTICED

Concentration on us, many times, heals family members in ways that are hidden from our views. We have come into these lives perfectly suited to "souls" from past lives to have the chance once again to find the love and heal the disagreements, settle our personal wars, and leave the earth with our mission done. If not completely done, we are always making progress. These opportunities to heal lifetimes of Emotional Rags further develop the Christ that lives within. Fortunately, this is not a sentencing, but an opportunity.

PROGRESS NOT PERFECTION WORKS!

We may not heal all of what we need to heal with our families, but it is better to look at progress, not perfection in this endeavor. *We have time. They have time.* Time is not the enemy. Just know that time is on our sides. We can take the gift of time in increments. And, with the healing performed in increments of time, we experience increments of peace. There will come a time when we lovingly and attentively show up, and are healed. At that time, we will be able to totally "let it be." Moreover, we will intuitively know that we are complete by the peace that we are feeling. At that time we will have eliminated our own Emotional Rags. We are ready to embark on a higher road, a more useful and fulfilling earthly contract. We begin by just showing up to our next right thing. *We have earned our wings.*

So, families that "rag" together cannot stay together, unless there is no sign of healing. But there does come a time to move on if we learned the lesson. We move on with a great deal of wisdom, love, and respect for the lessons and the journey we have completed. It is best to love them so much that we let them be. We let them be without anger, hurt, or resentments. Loving under all circumstances gives everyone the freedom they need to get where they need to go.

A PERSONAL STORY OF EMOTIONAL
RAGS TO SPIRITUAL RICHES

A birth family, extended family, close friends, comrades at work and/or people, in general, that are in close contact, cannot stay together, if they are "ragging" about each other.

In other words, if the past cannot be left alone, as well as the future, family and friends will stay in the Rags of emotion. So here is my story of how I held on.

Personally, I tried to hold on tight to my family, friends, and my loved ones, and found that as I grew spiritually, I was losing them. I tried with a vengeance not to let that happen. I found as we all do at some point… it just does not work to hold on to those who no longer want to be in our lives. Many would call this a family feud or an unfixable situation because of the strong willed people involved. But it was for me a wake-up call when I finally realized that there were members of my family that just did not like me. Love, yes. Like, no. Being told I was loved was nice to a point but needing to be shown was a more important step that I was not getting. In the back of my mind and deep in my intuition I knew this was true but just could not face it. So I continued to gift, visit, and stay upbeat with the family that never contacted me or when they did it was not to ask questions about my life but to listen to theirs and talk about the weather. The conversations were empty and the phone time was short. I did hear about my shortcomings, my lack of understanding, and things that one family member was assuming I had done to get the success level I had worked to have. Still, I did not let go and then one day it occurred to me that I was not liked. I shared my feelings and started the process of letting be so that I could get to a state of peace since I knew I needed to let go.

The Emotional Rags arose and I found some fear in letting go. I would say to myself, "But they are my family." But were they? I was not valued in the family and yet I kept holding on to the illusion that they were my core. Not so. I was afraid to let go, I was in fear of becoming lonely and being alone. But, I was already lonely and alone having them in my life. It became clear that I had to start developing a good solid relationship with myself and be authentic and transparent enough not to let anyone or anything compromise my new found truth. I was being tolerated for my changes but not loved in a way that would support who I had become. The family that had been with me was no longer in my court. *I had changed.* I was no longer an emotional rag. I did not need saving and I was not willing to fix anyone anymore. I had never fixed anyone anyway. My ego just told me I was helping to fix multiple family problems.

THE FIXING STARTS WITH US NOT THEM OR THEY
That was an illusion, as my family and friends were fixing themselves to the degree that they were comfortable. And, I knew that I was making them uncomfortable. They just could not champion all my changes. Fortunately I had come far enough into my own path that I was not resentful.

There was a new dawn approaching, and I was meeting like-minded people wherever I went. *They got me.* They knew how I was feeling, and what I was talking about. They were having the same issues with their old birth families and friends. We always attract those we need and those who will mirror our lives right where we are. And by attracting like-minded people, we get the opportunity to drop our old Emotional Rags and be authentic and truthful as to where we are, what we need, and the path we are traveling.

LETTING THE ONES YOU LOVE GO IS VERY LOVING
It did come to me…how could I be so insensitive to let them go…and for many years I just could not. And in those years, I talked to them about the same old things, the same old past, and listened to their same old issues. *Why not? I loved them.* It took some time but after hitting bottom with the intuitive feeling that enough was enough, I started doing some acceptance steps and then letting them be. I was freely released from old conversations, and the past that was still their NOW. There was a calm that came over me. I was relieved, grateful, and in the realization that I was out of the family of birth lesson. I loved them and would hold them in my prayers and good thoughts but I was no longer held captive by people that did not know me or like me.

BLESSINGS COME BECAUSE OF NEW INSIGHTS

Today, my Riches are around them NOW with new insight. I am there to only listen. My suggestions are of no value in my outdated friendships and family connections. I have tried hard for years to keep my family intact. I wanted to because I thought it was my job. In other words, I got transferred to a new job with benefits. *Me. What did that mean?* Then, it finally came to me that loving others extravagantly in the NOW meant living on purpose. I meant to ask for nothing in outcomes, and just kept showing up and supporting positive changes. In other words, not expecting others to understand me was a big bundle of Riches.

I have to admit that it was definitely lonely, when friends and family started dropping off like flies. I held on until they let me go. I somehow knew that was the best thing to do. Intuitively, I worked with spirits and my guides. The timing was not mine. It never would be because my timing was always hurry and let's get it done. My job was to keep showing up and to love them, and just be there. However, in one instance, I had to let a family member go. I was not able to even listen anymore, and what I kept hearing was that it was not my job to fix anyone. No judgments were needed on my part, and no resentments were formed. If there was a judgment or a resentment, I did not hold on long.

OPENING UP TO A NEW LIFE

In order to be open to the ongoing rebirthing of my life and the messaging that was trying to come through, I could not be clouded with anyone else and their lessons. I realized that it did not even mean I owed an explanation to the verbal abuse and accusations that I received. The sibling was released and I was not the one who decided on that outcome. It came through my heart as the most loving thing to do for us, even though I was not in control of the final outcome. Even today I sometimes want to pick up the phone but I don't. If I am supposed to someday, I will. Loving unconditionally sometimes means stepping aside, so that the one you love gets to have his or her journey, without interference from other family members such as myself in this case.

THE HIGH WATCH HAD MY BACK

After letting go, I needed to return to and stay present to the high watch to make sure I was connecting with my own journey, and not someone who was still stuck.

Someone can hold you hostage with that word called "love", and tell you that they love you. It can be an emotional trap because when you realize they don't like you, they do not have the kind of healthy love. It finally becomes okay to step out of that ring of fire, into a cool pond created through the still small voice that lives within all of us to take the sting away. This is yet another example of a set of Spiritual Riches, in which Emotional Rags are replaced with simple, plain accessible knowledge for which we are finally ready.

I knew that my Emotional Rags could only reappear, if I allowed them to. I chose not to react to those things anymore. I wanted the Riches. I had done the work, and did not want to go back to those Emotional Rags that made me miserable.

When you face God head on, there is no turning back. We may try, but we know 'way too much to pretend we do not know what we are doing. And, when you look at God, and see him in the face of your family and friends, you end up seeing only the "best of the best" in yourself and in them, even if the relationships have become estranged. Life remains rich.

THE EGO IS POWERFUL ONLY WITH OUR PERMISSION

It may seem odd to say or hear that the only time we will ever have full power is when we are not under the constraints of our ego. At first this can sound very strange. We need our ego, right? We have to make important decisions right? The ego at its best is a great help to get us out of the way of an oncoming car or to save a swimmer from drowning. In our early evolution the ego kept us alive and well by knowing what to do and how to do it instinctively. But we have evolved and the ego has become an exaggerated source of constant messaging about the past, present, and future all rolled into many insane thoughts going all at the same time. How easy it is to find ourselves spinning with many answers and really never getting the one we need. It seems that the ego has taken on the battle cry for all the lessons we are learning when it comes to judgment, resentment, and anger management. It wants to always be right in a very convoluted and confusing way. The chatter is constant and it gives us little peace especially when we are in need of important life changing decisions. There is a fix that has proven to be effective and one that works: letting go of the chatter by learning the art of settling down, which allows us to contact our Higher Conscious Self. By doing so, we become ONE with the message, ONE with the Source, experiencing no separation by letting the ego run wild with a multitude of thoughts. By learning the various ways of shutting down the ego we find that the persistent voice in our head that demands to have its own way loses to a more concrete heart-directed answer. And that finds us rather peaceful and confident that we have made right decisions with our life. We will have the victory but the battle returns when the next challenge is in front of us. That is, until we start remembering to bypass the chatter more quickly and let our soulful selves listen for the heart-directed answers.

KNOW YOUR TRIGGERS TO ACTIVATE THE EGO

Drama is the sly game the ego likes to play when we are not watching. When there is a life challenge, and the ego starts up with a series of questions and statements that have nothing to do with the situation, except the fact that they could be related if we really let this force go, the mind takes over. We are quiet and pondering and BAM the ego brings in the fear, the resentment, and the anger about what we need to do. We are faced with that family of the "Should and the What Ifs" that we are trying to stay consciously away from if we have had the success of taming our unhealthy ego. Just as before with the last big deal in our life or so we thought, we find ourselves spinning once again with so many thoughts. We again start to conjure up fearful conclusions to things that have not even happened. But with practice at living in the NOW we can dump these Rags for the Riches and we will find that we are changing the way we think like a well-tuned automobile that shifts without a sound.

So, the question is, in our own defense, have we ever given our egos permission to be such renegades? We get caught in moments that have so much to say about something, and yet, many times nothing. Our breaths are stifled, and we are ready to defend, attack, and defend our own outlandish actions as reactions. So, the quick lesson is not to give our egos permission to control our conversations. In other words, stop the monster before it gets out of control. And, the only way to do that is to release our egos quickly, privately and with affirmative statements like: "You have no control." Breathe deeply, and you will be able to catch your truth, and release all that is not really relevant to you. *The chatter will subside.*

We let the tiger out of the cage because we left it unlocked. It is difficult to stay on a continuous high watch. But, with practice and pain, and then, practice again, it becomes an automatic reflex. *Listening is always the key to a shutdown.*

Impeccable with our words is not part of our mantras, when our egos are hard at work. We would like to think we are doing our best, but, in reality, we are at our worst. Many times, we fear being truthful, therefore we try to stick to a few fragments of truth, but, truthfully, that truth is not an impeccable truth. Once again, our egos have been poised for attacks, and, as a result, they keep us under a spell of fear. In other words, we get caught in the dance of being seen and heard, all at the same time. This is totally insane. It causes us to experience uncomfortable residuals from the insane behavior. We have become a caustic combination of emotional outbursts, and a monkey running wild with insignificant pointless egoist chatter.

THERE IS A CURE TO HEAL EMOTIONAL RAGS

Emotional Rags recognized are the healing element needed to have our Spiritual Riches. It is a rebirthing, by going through a life lesson and changing our thought process to one that works with ease and a successful outcome. We get a new life out of the old life. *Just surviving no longer works.* We are here to learn a new way of thinking that fills our lives with hope, freedom, and authenticity. We are getting ready to understand what it will take to receive our rightful inheritance of Spiritual Riches. But most importantly, have we decided this is what we really want and we are willing to change the way we think. Are we at least willing to take baby steps that will alter our daily lives and give us more of who we really are?

The answer has always lived within us. There comes a time to let the Universe remind us of who we really are and if we do not let the Universe nudge us willingly, it still is difficult to miss the message. We can ignore it but we really do not miss it. It does take the will and new tools of change over time. Then there is that big word that is always a challenge… commitment. Or do we have to be really emotional ragged out and at such a low bottom, that we finally will commit? Or is it possible that we do not have to sink in to the dredges of total despair to get our wake-up call? It is different for all of us. Hopefully, we can see the light before we enter into our own cave of darkness.

"We want to be our change." This means we want to not only change but to be a change that is so comfortable and normal that after a while, we feel that our change is a normal and healthy way to live.

There may have been a time, when a quick fix made us feel like we were on track. The quick fix comes in many mind-altering drugs from alcohol to drugs to sex and on and on it can go.

When we are young, we feel as if there is no end to our lives and that we have lots of time. Learning in our youth what will shape us in our later years is a gift but life does catch up with us. We get a choice: stay where we are and keep doing the same things getting the same results or…embrace change. Embrace a new way of thinking and listening. The listening will always come first. I was at that crossroads, too.

A personal story:

FOR GOD'S SAKE! DON'T LET ANYONE KNOW WHO YOU ARE!

I have so many stories about my ego. And of course I do. I was my ego with a presenting self that was not who I was. Some of me came through but I kept many secrets from everybody. My ego was not my friend and I lived with this chattering menace that was my guide to deceive myself and others; a mentor who was always telling me not to tell anyone who I was. I had learned to protect myself -- from everybody. I was never taught in my younger years to be transparent. My parents were not transparent so they did not have the skills to teach their children. I eventually had to be self-taught. Once I began deceiving myself and others I had to keep the story going. With this kind of chatter, I always took things personally, and was not impeccable with my word. Therefore, I was not able to do my best. In fact, I knew I was not doing my best. So, I stuffed it into my lower consciousness, and when this fact surfaced, I drank. I could finally forget and become totally someone else. When I look back at those times many years ago, I cannot help being embarrassed. I ask myself, was that really me? It was.

Taking this behavior back into my early years, as a child, I was taught behaviors that covered up everything. My family was all about hiding the truth. It was absolutely crucial that no one ever find out what was happening at 1643 Shangri La Dr. My parents who had taken on becoming Jehovah's Witnesses had a lot to hide. It started with smoking and being prepared for that surprise visit from a Witness. The all-alarm sounded and my brother and sister and I went into a full court press to hide ashtrays, the cigarettes and then to spray the Glade everywhere in the house. The doorbell would ring, and the house smelled like a car with a hundred Spruce Trees dangling from the rear view mirror. The all-alarm also was to cover up any despair, mental illnesses, and abuse. It felt as if we were trained seals.

The goal was to hide this family and its life from everyone. It worked for the most part but not with our neighbors. It was a screenplay of horror waiting to be written. The 24/7 screaming and swearing and yelling never ceased except for a short time in the late evening until early morning when my father was asleep.

As result, I was well-versed in hiding who I truly was. It almost seemed normal but the hiding made me very insecure and withdrawn. My self-esteem was almost nonexistent. I was a shadow of a person. And, as I grew older, and into my teens, I found out that I was different when it came to my sexual orientation. I said different because at that time I was not expected to be or think about anything but what society was calling 'the norm'. I had a sexual attraction to boys. I hid that, too. I never even admitted that to myself, until years later, after I had married a woman.

When my truth finally surfaced, I hid that too and I blamed my marriage, not my sexual orientation. But, truthfully, there was nothing wrong with my marriage except I was not supposed to be married to a woman with the feelings I had toward men.

I was married to a wonderful, beautiful girl, who was very attentive to me, and who was very much in love with me. To this day, I am grateful for the time I spent with her and the love that she gave me. It was the first time I had ever felt that kind of love. Today, I have let it go but my heart still can feel deeply sorry for not understanding myself well enough to stop a marriage that should have never come about in the first place.

I NEVER LIKED ALCOHOL BUT I
LIKED WHAT IT DID TO ME

I never enjoyed alcohol. Whenever I tried a drink to be social I got sick. One drink and I was in the bathroom. But with self-training, I started to drink. I realized that it made me feel different and once I could tolerate alcohol I used it to calm my fear, tell my story, and become who I was sexually. I also did some bold, stupid things while drinking but that is another book.

YEARS OF EMOTIONAL DRINKING STOPPED WORKING

I crossed the line and I know the day I did so.

There came a time when my daily drinking habits were not satisfying me anymore. *I had a choice.* And then again I really did not have much of a choice if I wanted to have a life. I was at the bottom of bottoms. Morning drinking and not showing up to work or anything else had finally stopped me dead in my tracks. I needed help. I wanted help. I asked for help and had a friend drop me off at a 28-day treatment center for drugs and alcohol. Twenty-eight days was not the cure but the sobering reality that I had a great deal of work to do if I wanted to stay sober. It was a very fragile time as I knew no other life but the one I had been living with alcohol. I left the treatment center with a few tools and it was time to face a world where I was void of any coping mechanisms; a world that I had lived in for twenty years with my coping mechanism being alcohol. I needed to first address my drug of choice, and then, the rest would follow, if I wanted to stay sober. It was recommended that I start going to AA.

It was a good recommendation as the Twelve-steps of Recovery that are taught at all the meetings changed my life. The Big Book told me that I was not alone, and the members of AA supported my efforts to sober up.

WITHOUT MY DRUG OF CHOICE…MY EGO RUNS WILD

Without the alcohol, my ego chattered away, and I could not find any way for me to shut it down. In order to stay sober, I had to follow the program to the letter. Surrender was first on my list, and reading the Big Book came next, along with securing a sponsor. A sponsor in AA is someone who a recovering alcoholic sees on a weekly basis. Sponsors have been sober for a long time. They are in service to those, who have a desire to stay sober. In addition, sponsors guide addicts through the recovery process by suggesting things (methods and techniques) that can help them remain sober. Ultimately, sponsors love you, as do many of the serious people maintaining their sobriety, until you can love yourself.

Next on the agenda of my new life was to stay sober for 24-hour increments, go to meetings, and call my sponsor, if I wanted to drink. And, of course, I wanted to drink. *I was raw.* My ego would tell me that it was OK to have just one drink. But just one drink I had learned would kick in the disease again and off I would go to craving alcohol again. At that point the disease kicks in and the alcoholic drinking and behaviors are worse than before. I know because I did not sober up for long before I tested the waters again thinking I would be okay. Before long I was drunk again.

Now I had two big problems - staying sober and living sober. But, in time, with good AA direction, great support and attending to the Principles that I was learning with AA I was getting better. I had managed to put in some much-needed time in sober living and was improving my mind, body and spirit. *What a good feeling that was!*

It was so good that, unfortunately, I drank again. I celebrated my recovery. I was falling back in the Emotional Rags of alcohol and losing my connection that I had found in the Spiritual Riches that I had so enjoyed.

My ego kept telling me that I was now spiritually connected and that I no longer needed to worry about staying sober one day at a time. My lesson was over or so I thought. *What a mess I was in!* My ego, and its protective false ways, had a grip on me again. The next thing that happened was a return to reality after I took a job that was impossible to save. I became despondent, drank excessively and ended up with a nervous breakdown; my back had two herniated discs and the pain medication and the huge amounts of alcohol found me in a full-blown nervous breakdown.

After going through days of hardly knowing where I was or who I was, I began to surface with the help of my best friend's parents who came to help me. I tried to stop drinking but could not as I was so sick and detoxing made it worse. The wonderful people who came to take care of me did not encourage me to stop drinking. They were not totally aware of my almost fatal disease. It took many months to become sober again. *And, it was much harder than it was the first time.* That was over 16 years ago. I was on my knees before God to take this obsession away with such a committed force to do so that I was relieved. The lesson was over and I have never even considered picking up that poison for me again. My ego can no longer talk me into anything around alcohol.

When becoming aware of the power of the ego, there is a Higher Conscious state of help to call on. *I found the God of my understanding.* I became the truth of who I really was, and began showing up to the life I was meant to live. I have learned so much about what works. Now I continue to learn what is needed. My life is full and rich and totally connected today. If alcohol hadn't been the culprit, I would not know what I know today. Thank you, alcohol! Thank you for every drink I drank. Thank you for all the mistakes. Thank you for taking me to the bottom of the abyss so that I could look up and have the desire to be on the crest of a mountain top. That is how it works. Alcohol was my biggest lesson to get me on track for the life I have today. The Emotional Rag that brought me to my Spiritual

Riches. And as I came to believe the truth of who I really was, I saw that my journey was to be amazing and it is *Amazing!*

THE TREASURE HUNT BEGINS AND IT IS NOT FAR AWAY

When enough is enough. When we want what we want, and we know that there is something out there greater than anything we have ever thought we could have, we are tapped on the shoulder, stopped in our tracks, and/ or confronted with enlightenment. Spiritual Riches begin with addressing our lives as they are NOW. When NOW becomes the most precious energy we could ever obtain, we are finally on to something big. This is what masses on this earth all covet, but it can only happen in the NOW. With our NOW comes the rest. Our good fortune and future arise during our NOW moments. During this time, we finally realize that we are here to live life fully, abundantly, openly, and with ease.

Does this mean we will be without problems or challenges? Are we to live as if there is no tomorrow? No, who could; in fact, there is a tomorrow, and there will be challenges and situations that will keep us growing in the right direction. The question is always, do we want to grow, change, and find more in our lives that we could do or have? Or are we shut down and content to not look into what could be next? Without challenges, there will never be opportunities, and opportunities are what we ultimately seek even when we are not aware that we are doing so. We want to discover the NOW. We are always aware in our own unawareness. It is our nature to know what is going on in and around us.

GIVE ME COMFORT OR…GIVE ME COMFORT

We want to become comfortably in-tune with our thoughts, and those times when we don't even realize that we are looking. If we look back, we will see that our quest is always to find comfort in our homes, jobs, and relationships. Why wouldn't we want a way of living that actually works?

ONCE AWARE WE GET THE NUDGE
OF THE SHIFT GOING ON

These new insights are different. They tell our story from the inside out with more depth and with a life of more purpose. They are not charged with the pity of Emotional Rags, but they do light up a path that up, until now, we were missing. There will be recognizable moments that we feel almost like we just got beamed up.

The strain is gone. There appears to be some clarity. We are peaceful and not even trying. The help is in all the corners and cracks of the universe. *How did we miss this before? What were we thinking or, better yet, not thinking? Could it be we were not ready until NOW?* We are once again on time to have the opportunity to have the answers to any of the Rags that are basically history. We are on the other side of a rag that we walked through and we are now ready to have the Riches that we so deserve. The awareness comes when we are attuned to seeing the light of our progress, and then, moving towards this natural, universal ONENESS that recognizes we did not do this alone.

We learn to listen. We feel a tap on our shoulder. We actually are willing to seek help and listen. We know that we are feeling the enlightenment when we sense a trust that we have never had before. And oddly enough that trust is first found in us. We are in the beginning of a new way of living. And as we move into this new dimension, the teachers appear with the tools of our new way of keeping our Spiritual Riches.

Our words begin to make more sense to us and we do not question our impeccable truth or the truth of others. We see the souls of others, not their flaws. Our actions will focus on the next right thing, as we silence the chatter of an unhealthy ego.

OUR INTUITION IS FUNCTIONING AT THE HIGHEST CAPACITY

We all have the gift of intuitive living. We are born with it. There are times we use it and times we do not. But at this stage of experiencing our Emotional Riches, we are running on all cylinders. There will also be a new recognition of the God of our own understanding. Call this energy what you like but the connection becomes strong within us. Fear will not perforate our consciousness, rather, there will be an awe of the Power we now possess. This Power allows us to create the life we had been hoping for. This Power lives within us. This is the loving presence of the God we have always been seeking. One without vengeance, one of loving kindness, one that helps us help ourselves. Now we live with this God and this God lives within us. This energy always has been but now we are ONE.

GETTING IT! THE QUESTIONING IS OVER...WE GOT IT!

There may be some of us who might find the next set of thoughts hokey and Pollyanna-ish. This is understandable if we have not really felt the entirety of the energy that is rightfully ours. But if we are in the enlightenment or far enough along that we can see it all coming, these thoughts will be worth knowing.

During this time of getting it, we realize that we have always needed a better understanding of this loving entity that we finally recognize. So there is a word or energy or a piece of nature that others call the God of our understanding. So the dreaming and the wonder and the fantasies, friendly guides and angels, along with loved ones who have gone on...that are in constant vapors around us and not 1000 miles away. *We feel them once the fear of knowing that they are with us is not a fear or a fantasy.* We are intuitively connected to them because we are finally open to the fact that we are not the only thing happening in our own energy. Our ego which has kept chattering endlessly with messages to distract us is somewhat silenced. At least, silenced enough to allow our listening heart to overpower the intensity of crazy messages of fear, resentment, anger, etc.

THE MIRROR IS REFLECTING BACK A WHOLE NEW IMAGE

The energies we seek, and the energies we choose, are the energies we become. This is our full length mirror and it is pleasant to look into it to see ourselves looking back.

Our old fears of a vengeful God disappear. Fear was our God and love took that God away to give us a new Higher Power. One that is co-creating in our lives. We are no longer judged, and punished by our Higher Power. Our God illuminates our levels of love. In other words, we no longer live with a God of pain, suffering, and wrath.

A DAY OF THE END OF WHAT WE WERE TOLD

So others have to live with fear to have good lives. Okay. In the life of enlightenment there is no fear and no need to be ruled by old church laws and painful church doctrines.

THE CHURCH COULD EXPOSE FEARLESS
LIGHT, HOPE, AND JOY

If we would love Spiritual Centers to sing, dance, and commune the love and freedom of the Universe, they are out there. They are not judgmental with their members walking around with a frozen smile assessing others. They are not fearful of showing themselves as who they really are. This is a Center that is open and affirming. This is a Center that gives a way of life that is not to be noticed, controlling or recognized for its material wealth and riches.

LET THAT LIGHT SHINE THROUGH, IT LIVES WITHIN YOU!

Times have changed. Pious church members are moving on to another level of understanding as they transition. They are lovely people and did their best as they prepared themselves to die from the day they thought that there was only one way to save themselves from a set of pearly gates.

However, we are in an historical time of truth when it comes to the life we are here to live and how we are connected. We are finding that this light that lives within is the God we have searched for.

THE LIGHT HAS OBVIOUSLY EXPOSED THE DARKNESS

There is so much light exposed in the universe, at this time, that the darkness is totally exposed. It may appear to be frightful, but, in reality, it must be exposed. The light is the goodness that has always won, and will continue to do so. It is our responsibility to allow the loving consciousness to come through. The more goodness that seeps into the universe, the more armor is needed to overshadow and destroy what is not the truth of mankind. *We are the light*. And, we have the honor to be the warriors of truth who show up in the NOW. We are the Spiritual Riches that come out of letting go of Emotional Rags. Our Rags go first, and the rest just IS. If we look at the history of mankind, and its connection to the universe, we will note that, under all circumstances, goodness always wins. But, with our light, we have joined forces with the Spirit of God that gives us the freedom to be who we really are. By exposing our real selves comes with it the uniqueness of Spirit. The artistic and amazing way that creation works to make all things different yet still connected. With our realization of a ONENESS of all things including humanity, could this be the key to the peace we are all in search of? If this started with us and the way we think, we would be changing the world one thought at a time. Energy travels at speeds unbeknownst to us as it has been already documented that healing thoughts can heal the sick thousands of miles away.

THE PEACE WITHIN COMES FROM LIVING OUR RAG
Personal Story:

I was lost, as a young man, so it took a long time to arrive at the "awakening state of a higher consciousness." But, looking back, I now see why it took so long. The timetable I was on was right on schedule. Fear was my biggest enemy. I was afraid of dying at Armageddon: God's war that is destined to eventually come and destroy the earth. At that time, all will die, except Jehovah's Witnesses. Then, there are those feelings – my attraction to boys. Oh, my God! I was for sure damned NOW. And, then there was something that I knew was wrong. I told stories that put me out of the limelight so no one would find out my deep, dark secrets. This was the beginning of my many Rags. My Riches, at this point, may seem odd to most, but they worked for me. I got married, and then, I left the marriage, after finally telling another person that I was gay. I started going to gay clubs, and, during my first time out, as a gay man, I ended up staying in my car for an hour, trying to get the nerve to go in. When I finally did go in, someone grabbed my crotch in the coatroom. I proceeded to throw up, left, and did not return for many weeks. The key for me was to arrive with a few drinks under my belt, which I did.

I was finally accepted somewhere. There were people, like me, who were openly gay, and there were those, who were still hiding. Those in hiding were not open and honest about their lives. They sneaked into back doors, just like me. And, once in that environment, they were free to be themselves. *Me, too*. But, it wasn't until I drank beer, and more beer, and then, some more. Now, I was ready to interact. The alcohol comforted me. While intoxicated, I was likely to say and do anything.

I went home with many boys over a period of about a year. Then, I ran out of "unknown guys" to have sex with. Truthfully, I didn't fully understand anything about having a serious, committed relationship with anybody. *Why?* Well, because I never had one with my own family. Therefore, I was not capable to of having a good marriage. I was just interacting with them for sex. It was the pre-AIDS era, and thankfully, I was spared from contracting the life-altering disease. I was free – totally free -- and could not wait to get back to the bar every night to drink excessively, and hook-up with men. *I finally felt desirable and normal.* All my life, I felt out of sync – a real oddball. But, not anymore. I was no longer separate from others. I was one of the guys. I was ONE with a community that accepted who I was. Those were my first Riches, and I needed them. There was no mistaking what I did, or how I did it. I had to come out, and I did in the best way possible for me.

There are a number of ways to change our thought processes, but it starts in that moment – the NOW. And, in order to keep the momentum progressing in the right direction, we must pay careful attention to what we say, and what we listen to. In other words, we need to learn how to show up to our treasure hunts, in order to claim our Spiritual Riches. Here is how it can begin to work.

KEEP IT SIMPLE *JUST SHOW UP!*

First things first, always commence a new beginning. It is living in the present moment, in the showing up process. It is a time of immediate reflection on how fortunate we are to have a way to look at what is stepping up to be the immediate next right thing.

I must admit…humor got me through many difficult times. It got me through some rough times where I threw my hands in the air, rolled my eyes and laughed instead of crying. Our humor will get us through anything. When life gets so absurd why not laugh at it. As that's when it starts getting better because it takes us off our pity-pot. Everyone can learn to laugh at themselves (i.e., we discover our zipper is down and has been for eight hours or we have static cling in the crotch of our gym shorts and everyone is hysterical as we pull it out and the shorts snap back showing everything we own). *Oh well, I guess it's time to just take it and be human.*

How serious can we make our lives? How intensely can we live out our days? Do we have more drama than a daytime Soap? Living our lives wanting to live instead of having to live or trying to live makes our days so much easier. If we live in our NOW moments with the people in front of us, our humor and everyday life lightens up. Our Rags are shorter, less intense, and more easily healed. However, we are not so important that we do not need each other. These are just tricks our egos use to make us believe that we are so important and self-sufficient that we don't need anyone else. Truth-be-told, we may think so at first, but, in all honesty, we need everything and everybody who is in front of us. We are not here to go it alone even if the insanity of our ego would like us to think so. The universe does not work that way, never has, and never will. It takes everything - working with us, for us to clear the way. We live in the big picture and we are the big picture for without all of creation there would be a hole and to date there is not.

AND UP POPS THE "WHAT IFS" AND THE "SHOULDS"

We all have guide help available, and there are times we need it more than others. What we begin to realize is that we are witnessing in our lives what is needed to bring us to our destinations. It is important not to get caught in imaginary, illusive thoughts (i.e., what we think is happening). We really don't know anything until we see what is in front of us. We learn nothing, can do nothing, and are totally misled if we let our egos throw the past at us (predicting a gloomy, and/or fearful future). None of it is ever true. The truth always exists in the NOW of our lives. We find that we need to be prepared to surface from lives of "what ifs" and "shoulds" if we want to tap into the present moment and the ONENESS of all things. There is energy all the time and it lives with us, for us, and has no separation in the fields of supply that it offers. Even in history, under horrific circumstances, we take note that goodness always wins. If we remember this, we can find immediate peace in our present moment.

A LIFE IS WAITING AND IT'S TIME TO LIVE IT!

There are many times we seem to be teetering on the edge of our next cliff, with no parachute to let us glide to our new life, yet there will always be a safety net to catch us. That is if we should, we jump out of fear and need the net of the Spirit to catch us.

We come to a thought that has finally put us in the present moment of our lives. We take the quantum leap and begin the journey of our lifetime. We are accessing our dreams. We are dressed in a garment of hope and trust. At this juncture, we intuitively know that we are on track and we know we have arrived.

The new life that is ready to embrace us can be smaller or larger than others, who have also taken the leap. This is not about others - this is about you. Our changed thought processes have set us up for changed lives. We all get to go the distance, and the distance is as far or near, as we are comfortable with. Many of us will say that we have felt the nudge. Some may even say it was an invisible nudge. Each nudge is a personal calling to begin. No two nudges are the same. We may not even recognize the nudge we get until later as we will someday take a look back. No matter how we get there, we are finally jumping. Thinking will never allow us to jump. It is when we stop thinking that we are able to scientifically respond to the movement. We will take a process and procedure that we have calculated works and add the Spiritual nudge to access this new life. This movement is much like a reflex of the knee. We are pushed into the arena that we are ready for. *We just move quickly without hesitation or very little fear!*

THINKING OBSESSIVELY WITH A FEAR BASE HAS CEASED

And, because thinking is not a true motivator, we have little-to-no fear, which is good. Fear does not even come into play, as our reflexes take us to the next levels of following good, orderly direction. We have leaped into the unknown. The contract is satisfied and the deal is done. Now, the real fun begins. We are in the flying high, and life has become a daring adventure yet experienced in a safety zone of the ONENESS principle.

Everything around us is for us and we are for it. *The fear is gone.* This becomes a spiritual gift that can only be explained by those who have stopped being motivated by fear, and taken the fearless jump into the next levels of their lives.

WE ARE MEETING A SACRED CONTRACT FACE TO FACE

We are surrounded with help from guides, loved ones that have gone on, and a Higher Power. We get the clarity that we have asked for. It becomes a pleasure to walk our talk.

Some will tell us, "It won't be easy," but was it easy living in fear and lack? And for whom is it not easy? With fear in the voices of our neighbors, they are still searching for what we have found. Everyone gets a chance to have it.

By letting go of the fear, we find ourselves surrendering with greater ease, and without the ego telling us that we are weak. We will actually find that surrender is our greatest strength. In losing our control, we are finding we are in control. Surrender and release provide us with the right to understand what is being channeled through our heart and is the best thing for us. The uneasy feelings in our stomachs have dissipated. We are no longer under the influences of unhealthy egos. Surrender has, once again, become the key to change.

SURRENDER IN THE FACE OF OTHERS IS OUR STRENGTH

What if we surrender in front of others? Isn't that a sign of weakness and so our ego chants? What do they think of me? Do I appear weak? Our egos would love to gain back control and run our thinking minds like a tree full of chattering monkeys. If we were to not buy into our chattering ego and observe what it is chattering about...we would find no truth but a lot of fear. And we do not do fear anymore and if we do it is quickly caught. We become so in-tune that in the egos chattering, resentments, fear and anger are easily discarded. We want to and have become, aware.

SPIRITUAL WARRIORS ARE READY
FOR SACRED CONTRACTS

Spiritual warriors, who walk the walk, are quick to make decisions. *But do not judge those who are judging them.* New found wisdom allows freedom of intuitive messages from our Higher Self and there is no need to join in the lessons of others. We are Warriors of love. We are on the earth to give away our greatest gifts be they big or small. Our path is now defined and we are allowing our lives to unfold for the greater good of others.

THE EGO NEEDS TO BE CONSTANTLY TETHERED

We will be going along smoothly and easily and yet our egos, out of the blue will want to jump in, challenging us to our Spiritual Riches and the way we are now thinking. At this point of ego entry, we will want to be aware that our egos understand that the ego can have a very addictive nature. It rallies hoping to be cunning and powerful. But caught red-handed by our present moment living, the ego loses its power.

SACRED CONTRACTS IN PROCESS
ARE A SHOW UP MOMENT

Truthfully, there is no right or wrong way to show up. Our lessons will be different and more surrounded by the need to stay present to our committed contract. We are definitely showing up to our new lives! We are the ones doing it. Nobody else is changing us. We are changing us! Finally! Our Emotional Rags can be appreciated for what they were, and then, let go. We have chosen new ways of thinking, and the results are always manifesting, sometimes quickly and sometimes slowly, but always manifesting.

SEVEN STEPS TO GIVE US THE POWER OF THE MOMENT:
1. SURRENDER
2. SHOW UP
3. ACCEPT
4. BE WILLING
5. TRUST
6. HAVE FAITH
7. SHOW GRATITUDE

We have touched on all of these but let's look a little deeper into what we already know lives within us.

This may sound easy - I can do that - I am that. But it is important to remember that if we were all that, we would not need numerous lessons of Emotional Rags to help us find our way. They are ways that are no longer chaotic, but peaceful. Ways that work, when we work at it. Lives that start to become what they are meant to be. Yes, it can be easy, but only if we are truly ready to embark on new thought processes. Our old ways of thinking have to die and be buried along with our past.

By tying ourselves to our pasts, and refusing to look towards our futures, we lose opportunities to have it all. We are not meant to have everything, but we are meant to have it all: all that we focus on; all that is part of our Sacred Contract and supports our contract. Everything we need will show up without issue. We will have financial, emotional and Spiritual support. Because we can have the entire, only component, having it all is knowing that we can and believing it with a deep trust.

THE AMBUSH OF THE EGO IS OUT OF A JOB
The ego is going to have a rough time infiltrating faith and trust. It just does not work. We can claim our strengths, and become stronger, because we have become ONE with something much greater than the chattering menace of an ego.

Surrender

So we had it rather tough growing up. We felt abandoned. We felt that we were not loved. Our brother always got the Fruit Loops and we had to be raisin counters and were always hungry...oh well. When we get caught up on what happened in our youth, our teen years, and our early 20s, we are nowhere even near our present moment. We are in our past -- a past that is gone and cannot be changed. And we may still have some deep seated resentments now and if they are not resolved, we might even keep them at the ripe old age of 100.

At 100 we may forget about the Fruit Loops and the raisin counting... because we may be forgetting everything, anyway. Our lessons are never over until they are over. It may take lifetimes to change the way we think, or if we are willing it may take a second of our time to join in our own present moment. This current lifetime we get to address some important changes to multiple gifts as our ultimate outcome.

WE ARRIVED TO THIS LIFE READY...BUT DID WE KNOW IT? Are we ready? We probably thought we were before we arrived. Upon rebirthing into this lifetime we find that we are ready to embark on changes that will give us new hope, new freedom, and a Higher Conscious Self. Most of us want to evolve to our highest levels and that is why we tune into teachings and nudges that are being published globally.

Eternal we are. It would be comforting to think that we could accomplish at least some of our goals as we walk through another lifetime of important and intense information that will access us to our Spiritual Gifts. They are always waiting for us to be ready.

Show Up

WHERE EVER YOU THINK YOUR NEXT
LIFE IS...YOU WILL GROW
We are part of an evolving Universe that is always changing and always growing. No matter what your heart tells you, growth will always be part of the journey.

Our past is our past. It is gone. It can only be a learning tool for the present moment, which naturally on its own has the option of building a successful, productive, and abundant future. The Now is our future in progress. Our good future depends on our NOW. This life can be so much easier by just showing up in our moment and doing whatever the next right thing is.

The questions always posed are, "What is in front of me?", "What is my next right step or action?" And then...no dilly dallying. Those who have aspirations to Higher Thought know to just do it! Just Show UP! No more waiting. No more pushing things aside. It becomes much easier to just address our NOW moments. Our future reaps the benefits and the rewards.

When we have not surrendered to anything, we find ourselves whining, stomping our feet, complaining, and feeling depressed, angry and despondent.

POTTY TRAINING IS NOT A FOREVER LESSON…IS IT?

It's okay to change our diapers and move on to the next level of potty training. Staying in the dependency of infantile baby tantrums is not growing spiritually. We are here to grow to a Higher Level, to recognize we are here to be ONE with a Power much greater than we are. There is a recognition that takes place in which we feel this ONENESS because we are accessing a pure and loving communication with our Higher Power. We need the tools to learn this lesson.

Yes, some of our past is frustrating, irritating, and maddening. But there comes a time when those hurts need to be addressed, defined, and gone… they have to go. If we are to move on to our next great thing, our next great experience and our next right incarnation, there comes a time when we are asked throughout our God Center to let it go. Our heart knows. We know. The Spirit knows. If we do, the hurts and discomfort we experienced will not be able to repeat themselves - unless we keep letting the voice in our head take over once again. That egotistical voice loves the drama and keeps the ego well-fed and keeps the soul in need out of rhythm with the only thing that can change a life successfully: the God of our understanding, a voice of truth that comes through perfectly when we listen. We are deaf until we have mastered the quieting of our ego and the listening to the heart.

HOW YOU ARE FEELING TELLS YOUR STORY

The truth becomes apparent by the way we feel. When we need to move on, adversity and change are REAL, an illusion of good things to come. We will need the gift of knowing to let go. There is no other way for the Spiritual Warrior to accomplish the battle with the ego. Opportunity will surface like a warrior on a white horse in a victorious battle. The ego and the heart, until tamed, make a vicious battleground. However, with attention to the heart, addressing opportunity in the NOW, we leave adversity behind. It's automatic. It will happen without trying and without struggle. It's the way of the Spiritual Warrior. It's the way to the treasure that has long awaited us.

SPIRITUAL WARRIORS KNOW THAT THEY KNOW

We are gifted with many Spiritual Riches once we win our battle with our willful ego running on its own without Spiritual supervision.

A Spiritual Warrior knows how and when to review a haunting past as a prerequisite to letting it go permanently.

The warrior in us feels when it is time. With learning the discipline to be quiet, and accessing the voice of stillness, we receive a defined message with authority and loving direction. This is not a fearful voice. It lives within us and co-creates with the God of our understanding to be in our best interest. Stillness always speaks. It is the Divine Light illuminating our path.

We come to believe with a certainty what is. The NOW moments are also recognizable as admission to what IS and then accept our moments for what they really are. There is no past and no future in the IS of our present moments. A Spiritual Warrior knows what this means.

ADMITTING AND KNOWING AND BEING HUMAN HELPS

Being human, having a spiritual experience, may find us still asking ourselves why. Knowing that our answers live within, taking ownership of quieting down once again for the guidance of our Higher Power is one of the Riches we can now call upon. We will access the NOW and let the days of old thinking and worn out habits dissipate and die. With this attitude and clear thinking, it is nearly impossible to be a victim. The self does display itself as a more peaceful Spiritual Warrior and is noticeably on track and a warrior of action.

PEDAL TO THE MEDAL OR SLAM ON THE BRAKES, WHICH?

The speed with which we surrender those years IS a time of growth and opportunity and will help us to keep making all the needed tweaks as they surface. Our big lessons seem to be done. The pedal to the metal is how fast we decide to change. Do we speed up or do we slow down or is there a need to slam on the brakes of change? If we are in our IS moments of the present, we will know. When we are stopped it becomes obvious that we need to slow down and allow the Universe to bring everything to order for us. If we need a good kick in the butt, we will feel being pushed off the next emotional cliff. We will know what to do.

Do we have to go it alone? No, not if we truly know that we are part of the whole of the ONE. Going it alone is a long arduous journey that ends either not working or working by default when others step in to help us. Our successes are everyone's successes and that goes both ways. Those of us who tune in and access the help that is available soar with lives of abundance and prosperity. We can humbly see how each person who is in front of us for whatever reason is our gift. No one need be left out.

Learning how to check in daily and listen to our still small voice finds us almost addicted to the clear messages that give us our NOW answers. We often may ask, "What took me so long"? But as we again listen we will be told why it took what it took to get us to where we are.

MISTAKES AND ALL, THE UNIVERSE LOVES US

Once again we will find a Universe that loves us and we will get to have as many false starts as it takes to get where we need to be to access a life of Spiritual Riches. Emotional Rags are just part of the journey. They are needed so that we know more about non-judgment of others as well as how to access our own self-love. When we are offered a choice and we do not change our thinking and our behaviors, we find that the pain of the Rags elevates pain. We are forced to stay stuck. In that moment of truth, we are offered a choice: either leave the pain or elevate the pain.

AM I REALLY HERE TO LIVE WITH EMOTIONAL PAIN? NO

We are here on this earth to have a better and better life. This was not intended to be a painful experience. What kind of a loving God or Universe would wish that on us? To have the life we are here to have we are required to show up. It will always be up to us. It will always be our choice. We make these choices in moments of present moment living. There is no one in the Universe who can ever fix us except our co-creative abilities that we develop with our Higher Self. We can call this anything that helps us understand that there is a power greater than we that provides us with all the life answers we need to have.

We may try to carry our burdens by ourselves and our burdens may want to even control us but in the end, the only way to lose this emotional rag is to align ourselves with our co-creative power, embrace our connection and become willing to accept this energy that is everywhere and in everything.

THE RISK TO SURRENDER IS NO RISK

It's not as risky to surrender as we might surmise. It may feel that way… as fear seems to always rear its ugly head when we come to a point of knowing that we need to let go and surrender our question to something bigger, higher, and more capable of helping us. And then we are back to that still small voice that is the God of our understanding coming through loud and clearly or quietly and penetratingly. By not taking what we think is a risk, we will never know, nor will we have our answer. We can keep trying, or we can retreat to our same old way of living and our same old results. It may take our first try or our second try or our 50th try. It is not how many times that we need to show up to make our surrender stick, it is that we stay focused and willing right to the end. The gifts await us in our surrender. The message is, "Don't give up!" Show up and let your life show up to you. We are in charge of our own surrender. It is a choice.

In the moment of surrender, the ego is caught off guard, stunned and dumbfounded, totally immobile and disconnected and unable to chatter. Our surrender saved a precious moment. We feel the ease and the peace and NOW know that fear had no strong-hold.

Accept

ACCEPTANCE HOLDS THE KEYS TO OUR KINGDOM

You hold the keys to your Kingdom… It is a Kingdom that we live in by the way we think. Acceptance of what is… is absolutely the key to making sure our kingdom is not taken over by a band of egotistical, runaway "Shoulds" and "What Ifs." They are always lurking but are powerless voices of the ego when acceptance takes center stage. The "Shoulds" are tied to the ego, totally unable to function if they are not consulted. Our emotional adversaries do not have the keys unless you hand them off. However, just know the ego wants those keys. The "What Ifs" keep hanging out with the "Shoulds". But we are in charge of our own Kingdom. We can raise our own bridges and make sure our walls are secure. The "Shoulds" and the "What Ifs" are no longer empowered by the ego and are not let in through our thoughts or our cunning ego that does not believe in acceptance. Acceptance kills the ego.

ADD A DOSE OF DRAMA AND THE
EGO WANTS PRIME TIME

In the course of a day in the life…we may find ourselves living in a daytime soap… Our World Turns into the Edge of Night. Starring the Eddie Ego and Thoughtless Thelma. Drama is always a key player in recharging the ego. And the ego is ready at a moment's notice to jump into our lives and take control of our thoughts with multiple layers of chatter. In a split second, even with all the Spiritual knowledge and awareness, the ego still is ready for center stage and taking control sending out messages of doubt and fear.

However, with acceptance of what is, we become accustomed to being on the lookout for this feisty drama queen. We are willing to do minimal reacting to people, places, and things. How much easier it becomes to live in the present moment of what IS.

AND WHEN WE DO NOT SLOW DOWN…
WE GET A LITTLE HELP

Sometimes it takes conscious effort to slow down. If we do not cooperate with our intuition, sending messages that we need to slow down, the Universe steps in and helps. Have you ever stubbed your toe and had to sit down? Did your back go out and make you stop everything you were doing? How about that cold that put you down for a week of rest and recovery. This slowing down period is nothing more than reminding us that our answers are wrong and the right answers are coming when we have relinquished control. We are blindsided by a chattering ego on an egotistical rampage leaving us unable to hear what our next right move is or what our answer to the current situation is.

CONTROLLING OUR THOUGHTS: TO BE OR NOT TO BE...

It may or may not feel odd that we got stopped right in the middle of an obsessive controlling thought that we are not willing to let go. But like all Emotional Rags, the Universe has a way to help us surrender if we recognize what is happening to us when we do finally get slowed down. It is a great time to claim protection...from ourselves. We later learn it was the only way we could have even hoped to be stopped. Any change of thinking whether it is surrender or the admission and acknowledgement of where we are is the start of healing. The Spiritual Riches await us. That is the future we are making in our NOW. We return to meditation and prayer and we listen.

PERSONALLY SPEAKING, SLOWING DOWN WAS NOT MY WAY

For years I have always had a difficult time when my life slowed down. I always felt like I was missing something. And I found out I was right. I was missing the time that I needed to just be. I was missing my chaotic running and scurrying about just to look and feel busy in a self-worthy way. I was like a robin always trying to get one more worm. And I would become so full of worms that I could not sing my way into spring even if I wanted to. I found through this valuable lesson that I did not need all those worms dangling in front of me. Just one at a time would do me well.

By finally slowing down I became much better prepared to show up for my next right thing instead of 50 wrong things. I would be exhausted because of my fast acting body that was following my fast and chattering ego. I realized I no longer had to be busy with being busy. How many times can you wash a car, sweep a floor, or cut your grass? How many times did I need to figure out my family, job and friends? I was living with an odd combination of guilt and the illusion of success. If I did not look busy, I was not productive. If I was productive I needed to be busier. At least I needed to look busier. Thank God there is a softer, easier, saner way. Today I breathe. Today I listen. Today I do not apologize for being tired or wanting to read a book, take a walk, or just sit and be. I am allowed to have all of life…not just the "watch me work…aren't I something else??" And as I write this I got a great big laugh at what I thought I had to look like for me to be accepted, valued, and loved. What a bunch of bunk!

My lessons with impeccable truth have continually reminded me to let my reading audience know that I have had my slips, too, in moving fast and furiously. But today with my antenna up and my intuition connected to my God Source, I usually catch myself. Instead, I value the still small voice that gives me my messages. I want to know what my next right thought will be so I can do my next right thing.

NOT EVEN THE ATHEIST, GOES
WITHOUT A UNIVERSAL NUDGE

We all have spiritual experiences on various levels in the journey. Be it the agnostic, the atheist, or the monk…we all get messages and they change our lives and our directions. The Universe is of ONE defined being so it makes sense to know that we are all connected. No matter what we say we are or what we say we know, we are all getting spiritual messages.

So here is a concluding thought on acceptance as an important Spiritual Gift to obtain: just know that when life throws us a few curves, and it will, accepting what IS, eases our emotional pain and gives us the courage to keep showing up. But most importantly, listening and showing up to the next right thing will always work under all circumstances. With this principle, our lives will stay on track and connected to the God of our understanding. We will find that we are living in the Oneness of Spirit and there is nothing we cannot do or have. This is an incredible Spiritual Gift.

Be Willing

WILLINGNESS (WILLING TO BE WILLING)

This thing called Willingness is about walking our talk. By showing up we become willing to walk our talk. It is a commitment that changes our life one day at a time. Without willingness, our talk and our walk are just not in sync. In the practice of cause and effect, there is no way we can cause a new situation to take place in our life if we are not willing to intentionally commit to it.

There are many times we may say we are willing but when the rubber hits the road…our brakes are locked and the only thing we are willing to do is to be unwilling. We are scared! We may not know it, but fear has found a crack in our energy field. We are so stuck and yet so ready for a positive change. We talk about it. We have quick starts. We over dramatize why we can't do what we said we would do. Because we just are not willing.

Trust

Willingness comes with Action to Engage. It is quite simple, but it has to be embraced fearlessly. Trust and faith work. Hope does not seem to work as it is not enough of an Action Step. Hope is future thinking. If we hope we will, most likely we won't.

By the acknowledgement of hope in the present moment we are already doing so. We have the faith in ourselves every time we commit in the NOW. It does not take desperation to change our world, it takes commitment.

Desperation is an unnecessary choice unless we think that we need this as an Action Step to get us motivated. But desperation does not come from the heart. Desperation comes from the head. Sometimes we make this move of desperation to motivate ourselves to find out only that this goal could have been achieved in a much shorter time with much less stress.

Have Faith

WHAT ABOUT THIS THING PEOPLE CALL FAITH?
Faith SIMPLY believes under all circumstances that we will not necessarily get what we so desperately want but that we will get everything we need. We do realize that when we are willing, we are actually showing a great deal of faith in our ability to listen, wait, and expect the best results.

Showing up in our daily lives becomes much easier! With willingness, we can have faith. With faith we can have the freedom of knowing that what we need is already taken care of. That is where patience sets in.

IT IS SO MUCH FUN TO *WANT* TO SHOW UP

Let's face the facts…we have to show up every day of our lives to something…why not show up to all we are and all we love? We can accept the inevitability of change or live fearfully losing freedom to feel how alive we really are. When we want to show up, we know that we are truly alive. Try it! Try wanting to be a part of it all! There will be times when change is blatant and there will be times when the need to change takes on a more subtle nature. But once again, we either decide we want to show up to the changes in front of us or we back away and lose the freedom that change brings. When one wants to show up with the necessary willingness to embrace change, there is a beam of light dancing in the window of our lives. It has always been there and always will be. Are we willing to stand in those rays of enlightenment or do we want to stay in the shadows of an old life that has been prepped for change?

WE HAVE A FULL TIME JOB THAT REQUIRES ONE THING

Our job is to recognize it and start listening. We will be led. This is how the Universe works when we have learned to listen and to be ready.

For many of us there have been many times when we were unhappy with our life's circumstances even when we had learned from past experience how cause and effect works. The Emotional Rags were evident, and we seemed to be repeating behaviors. We wanted change again. We may even have been asking everyone, again, what we knew intuitively to do. And again we were reminded that the person who always knows what is best for ourselves is ourselves. We always have the answers and as has been stated millions of times, by Buddha, "When the student is ready, the teacher will appear." At this juncture we are already teachable by just showing up. We ask "why?" to many questions including "why am I here and what am I to be doing?", and yet we always know deep within us our own answers. We know we want a better way to think and live, and we know it is available. Being willing, to the "What IS" in front of us, is a great, valiant start. It once again stimulates the Spiritual Warrior that has always lived within us. With this armor, we soon realize we are to be an open vessel that allows all the good to come in and then allows that which no longer works to be dumped along the way. Open vessels are transparent and authentic and absorb the truth that is messaging on a soul level.

WE HAVE HEARD IT BEFORE...IT IS WHAT IT IS

We become willing to experience the "IS" in our lives and we experience far more possibilities and realities than we ever did before. We come out of the IS with many possibilities to change into who we really are.

We get to decide what our day will look like. But more importantly we get to decide how our day is to feel. If we are experiencing untreated depression we will not know what or how to feel thus keeping our lives at bay. So decisions need to be made, be it a doctor's appointment, a meditation, or a prayer. But we are in need of action. Our life cannot unfold until we have recognized and treated depression whether it is clinical or brought on by life's circumstances. There are some who have a DNA issue with depression and are prone to periods of deep downward mood swings. However, in a world of ONENESS and availability to pure energy brought to us by the talents of the doctors who treat depression, we are encouraged to seek out this God-given care brought to us by the medical field. Once we are treated, we also have the spiritual tools as well as the benefits of science to help us rise above and beyond thoughts that are not part of our soulful journey. Our Emotional Rags of depression are the road to Spiritual Riches if we know what is necessary to treat a disease that can take our life away.

MY PERSONAL STORY

I was one of those people who had undiagnosed depression. From a very young age I was in a state of sadness. I always felt down and the low energy readings that I gave off were very detectable especially by other young boys and girls who were healthy. I was subjected to bullying. My depression was untreated until after I turned 45 when by accident I was being treated for what I thought was a heart attack when in reality it was anxiety and depression. I had suffered for years with low self-esteem and high anxiety. I found my fix to correct these feelings in alcohol. It was the only way that

I could be relieved of this intense and menacing disorder. Thank God I did not add drugs to the mix. It is a hard situation to try to explain unless one has been through the cycles of high anxiety and depression.

At times I found that I could not think clearly, make rational decisions or move to the next right thing. I was full of fear. Alcohol took the fear from me and added impulsive decisions that many times were wrong. I was always second-guessing myself. My work was always shrouded with a hyper blood-sucking energy that made me feel defensive and never good enough. The rest of any energy that was left I used to maintain a voice and a presence behind my illusive curtain. My presenting self was programmed to hide what was going on with me on a daily basis. People would not understand. They would judge me. They would find out that I was not good enough. The "they" were frightening demons, and if they ever found out that I was depressed and living an undercover life with alcohol would abandon me. Even with alcohol, I had been abandoned many times as a child and again as an adult. I had to keep my secret life under wrap.

Today I am free of the depression and anxiety. But it took being willing to be treated for it. It took willingness to stop the drinking and face my demons. And as far as the people I thought would not understand, surprisingly they did. And the ones that did not I found that I did…oh well. Many times it became common knowledge later on that they were fighting their own demons. How would I have known? I was so busy hiding mine. My life started getting better as I was sober and began the process of addressing one by one the many haunts of the past. I have to acknowledge how wonderful the Twelve Step Program was for me. I already was spiritual in nature, but the simplicity of doing the steps in order gave me what I needed as I embarked on a life without alcohol. Of course it was more than alcohol I was overcoming. I had stuffed years away in the back of my mind. The years were surfacing and I had the tools to allow me to address why I drank as I did.

When I found out that I had levels of anxiety and depression that were manifesting as heart disease, I remember telling the doctor, "I am fine. My life is good." Why was I having these feelings out of the blue? It was a family disease and my DNA was set up to take on the disease of alcoholism. It came through not only on my father's side of the family, but my mother's as well. My dad had been sick for years with mental illness. It was mental illness spurred on by drugs and alcohol. I began to understand why he did what he did and why he turned out to be what he was. He was hiding, too. But like him, I had to decide to take the next right step. He was not willing and lived a life of horrific depression, pain, and mental illness until he took his own life at the age of 63. He took his own life by jumping out of a 13 story assisted-living building. My compassion is ever so present as to what he had to endure all those years of being undiagnosed and trying so hard to live in a world that was foreign to him. I lived there, too. But at that time in medical history, he did not get the kind of care that could help. He was drugged and drugged again just to keep him quiet when he finally ended up in a mental hospital. No one knew at that time what to do for these people. And without alcohol in the hospital he was first admitted to, he was raw with untreated emotional scars. It had to be very scary for him. I was of little help as I was young and had been so abused by him that I was at a loss as to what to do. I followed directions and got him into a mental hospital as he had tried to commit suicide more than once. Today he would have had a better chance if he were willing to address all the horrors that kept him so sick for so long. So what does this thing called willingness have to do with my story?

ONE OF US IS READY FOR ANYTHING UNTIL WE ARE READY

There are daily tools that can put us on the cutting edge of finding our willingness and then keeping it. By learning the art of meditation and affirmative prayer we find that our old way of fearful thinking goes away. When we are willing to listen in our NOW moment, we find how willing we are to fearlessly move forward and then "stay in place" waiting for continued God-Direction to take us to our next right step.

By doing what is in front of us, no matter how big or how small, we will find answers coming through our Heart Center. The answers have always been there. We just need to be on time with willingness. It becomes time to recognize what we thought was our *problem*. That is really our *question*.

The answer will appear on time and at the right time if we just ask. It sounds easy but being patient is another story for most of us. When we get our answer we often will say, "Oh my God, that is a miracle!" Yes, at first it appears to be because we have never used this newly found ancient formula to solve our questions. And even if we knew about this formula, it takes us time just to continue to become aware. And sometimes we still have to go through a lesson of bottoming out. But once again walking through an Emotional Rag will give us our Spiritual Riches as long as we are willing.

It may seem strange that willingness is really all it takes, but those who have been down the path of living through their Emotional Rags will verify how true this is. That's what it takes to get the Universe in motion to answer and guide us into our next right thing. Once you have put willingness into practice, what was once thought to be a miracle suddenly sheds a new light. In the future living with willingness becomes more common place in our lives. Without discounting a miracle, it may be rightfully said that our miracles have been going on since the beginning of time and now we are recognizing that our whole life has been a lesson in how to accept the miracle. We are living and breathing in the vapors of Universal Understanding. We are ONE. What a gift to behold. That in itself is one of the biggest miracles for us to recognize.

MIRACLES WILL SHOW UP…AND YET AGAIN SO WILL THE EGO

So what happens when the ego takes its turn again right after you go through the last surrender of something that you needed? It does take some conscious effort to calm down the overbearing monkey mind of the ego. We have already determined that to listen we have to tame this pesky beast. We know the ego only has the control we give it. So what is the miracle here? Simply, we finally know and we are utilizing our new-found Spiritual Gift of Riches. We experience an inward calming effect that will take the place of the chattering ego. It is so calming that we can quickly hear that still small voice leading the way to our once mind-rattling ego that for years has kept us tethered to doubt and fear.

CHATTY KATHY AND DOUBTING THOMAS HAVE MOVED

In the continued effort to not let the ego get the upper hand, we turn to the one sure thing we have always had and will always have: our Higher Power. We will find once again that the answers to our questions are coming to us in the increments needed to get us to the final solution with all the other souls that are to be involved in our Spiritual Riches.

STAY TUNED TO THE RADIO AND
EVERYTHING ELSE AS WELL

The answers can come from almost anywhere. It may be a quiet thought or it may come through in a song on the radio. It could be on a billboard while driving home from work. Or maybe a long lost friend has contacted us for a conversation that contains the exact message we need to hear. And do not discount an article that we happen to pick up in a waiting room at a doctor's office where an out-of-the-blue message jumps out to our rescue. Nothing is by accident when we are present to our moments. When the ego is not in play, when we are in our present NOW moment, the answer comes and is on time.

Because we live in a world of ONENESS, our answers will continue to come right on time. This also reinforces that we are all in this thing called life together. It is like the planets, the moon and the sun, when left alone, move in perfect synchronicity. Timing is always right for the answers to our questions. When we KNOW finally, we will get our answers! We are saying an affirmation to the IS in our lives knowing that we will be taking in the answers with soulful intuitive direction from our Source and Supply. It is humbling in our moment of discovery to attest to a force that has such power and then to take it to the next level and realize that this Force lives within us.

Show Gratitude

GRATITUDE TAKES US TO OUR KNEES…OF KNOWING

No longer is there a need to get stuck in future or past thinking, let alone the illusion of what we think is happening in our NOW. Gratitude sets in as the still small voice of non-reaction takes over and guides us to solutions that we used to find ourselves lamenting over. It is a time of realization of how fortunate we are; free from the obsession of an egotistical mind. Life has changed and is so much better and easier.

The ego has lost its power. The agitation, high and lows, or fears of the "what ifs" and the "shoulds" are no longer with us in the form of preconceived doubt. The bag of tricks that the ego has used for years is empty and High Drama is a surfing channel that has gone off our flat screen. Spiritual Riches have given us programing that is more individually suited to our life and the life we are here to gift.

WE TRUST WHEN WE FIRST TRUST OURSELVES

Do you or did you not trust your parents? Do you or did you not trust your partner/spouse? Do you trust your employer and the people you work with? Or not? Did you or do you trust yourself? We can never trust anyone until we finally trust ourselves. If we want the ability to trust we must find out if we are authentically trustworthy. Are we transparent about who and what we are? Or are we living a life where we do not trust anyone because if we do the trustworthy lifestyle is mirrored back to us? And what does it take in our own lives to start letting others know us? With questions such as these we are in for a real wake-up call. And as all lessons…this is good.

It has been said that the best place to start is at home with who we really are. We are the only ones who can take on this very important self-inventory. Nobody knows us better and nobody can change the way we trust or do not trust except for ourselves.

Some easy questions to ask are, "Am I transparent enough to be truthful? Do I assume that everyone is out to get me? Am I afraid to let people know who and what I really am? Have I accepted myself in all areas of my life? That would include my strengths and weaknesses. Am I done hiding?"

With these few questions, we can assess our lives quickly. There may be some areas that we can answer affirmatively and others that we hang our heads over or ignore. But until we find ourselves, we will never be able to trust anyone fully. We will always doubt whether others have our best interest at heart. They are doing exactly what we are doing, not trusting.

If we are not willing to be open, honest and trusted, why would we consider that anyone else would? This is a time to have our own best interest at heart. We are the problem with trust.

Once we have finally been willing to take a good look at who we really are, or are not, we are ready to embark on a journey of transparency and authenticity.

By acceptance of all our good and all that we would like to change, we get closer to a ONENESS Principle that we will not be willing to lose. By accepting the next right thing with both the good and bad that we are... we are closer than ever to experiencing a ONENESS with The Divine. At this point we may come to an understanding and have an opportunity for willingness to open up and to start trusting others. When you know yourself so well, trusting others is no big deal because you are transparent and whole. Whatever they may say about you is true because you told them what your truth was. This becomes an exciting time of enlightenment. Who can hurt you now? No one.

The most important part of trust is not only admitting all that we are, but then just showing up to our lives every day as an open, truthful, authentic being. Because we are present with integrity we can trust others and be trusted. We attract safe trusting people to share our open ended story.

And if the time should arise when we need help with finding trust in another, it will never be a problem, but it will be a question that we automatically take to the still small voice that lives within us. The truth will show up because we have become truth. We are living truth, and we have learned to trust our intuition to guide us. We can accept that we have something bigger and better helping us. Our angels, loved ones, the great masters and guides are among us to channel information to help us in this lifetime. Never alone and always connected, we remain on high alert and allow our answers, sacred contracts and points of service to show up committed to listening.

GRATITUDE BEGETS GRATITUDE
THANK YOU VERY MUCH!

If life is not working…your way, how wonderful. What a great opportunity to be grateful. Life seems to be going along great and much is happening to make it better. What a great time to be grateful.

Gratitude knows that you know everything that is happening for you and to you is something to be grateful for. If there is strife, stress, and loss in your life, how in the world would you think that you could be grateful? Maybe you cannot at the time, but it comes later. We need change and upheaval in our lives to sometimes make us change for our own good. Stress is an indicator that we need to change our life and change our thinking. For this we can be grateful. Strife is annoying and hard to live through and as we change our thinking, we can find a way out. And this will be a better way for us in the long run. For this we can be grateful.

Loss is terrible for us to go through; loss of a home, a partner, a job, or a pet are all deeply tearful times. But if the home we lost becomes freedom, and the partner is one we have outgrown, this is not loss even though it feels that way at the time. And then there is that job we hated. We never liked it, but we were too afraid to quit. Our troubles were over when we got fired. Thank God something got us out of there. Now we can hopefully be willing to find a job we love. If a loved one or good friend or a pet must go on ahead of us, it is hard. We are left behind, but we get to see how it is done. We get to know that life does go on. And with loss comes a reality that we all are here for a short time and we need to honor the moments and make the best of it. Mortality sets in and for this we can be grateful so that we stop wasting time and start showing up to all we love in the moment.

Gratitude is all of the above. As we grow and learn and show up we get to be grateful in the moment. It's like cutting the grass or painting a room… we receive instant gratification and who does not like that? Be grateful every step of the way and when you cannot be grateful at least acknowledge that you may understand more someday and this is another way of being grateful.

WE ARRIVED ON THE PLANET AS A SPIRITUAL GIFT

When was the last time you asked yourself, "Why I am here and what am I to do?" Many of us have asked but we forgot to listen and when we did, we thought that the information was for someone else...but was it? That thought or message could not possibly be for me...I can't do that.

When fear of moving forward sets in because of self-doubt, we are unintentionally putting our life on hold. Our Higher Power is not sitting in judgment of our "I can't" nature and thus we are not judged, or are we? The only judgment will be self-judgment. We are not moving forward. We want change but only if we feel comfortable. So we stay where we are somewhat comfortable and later ask ourselves why we did not make the change. There have been two schools of thought on not accepting opportunity. One is if you do not, the opportunity will not pass this way again. Or we can ask again and see what happens. It is true that opportunity is always in front of us but timing is everything. We are not in this life alone. There are others involved in our opportunities.

THE HAND-OFF FROM RAGS TO RICHES NEEDS OUR CONSENT

Emotional Rags to Spiritual Riches is not something we get or that is handed off to us without our consent. We must consent to the process we have been talking about in the previous pages. To reiterate, willingness and fearlessness are a requirement in addressing the Emotional Rags so that we can move into the Spiritual Riches. No need to worry about the Healing component. Healing takes time but beginning to heal is where the first sign of coming gifts starts showing up.

It is my hope that by sharing this Universal wisdom others may find value and answers in the Rags they are living and walking through. Finding the life Riches is what makes us whole.

If one decides to retain some of these principles in this short, simple book, there will be noticeable changes in the way life IS. Anyone can have the Riches. But we all have to walk through the Emotional Rags to fully understand that we are living in the Riches.

So the Rags to Riches story can be for anyone. We have the answers within...but there are times when we need another human being to validate our feelings and thoughts. At the end of all my classes I suggest and nudge the following: If you can remember just one thing in this session that will make your life better, please remember one thought... Just show up to the next right thing and you will be amazed at the transformation in not only your thinking but your life experience. Keep showing up and you will be more than fine.

Showing up to life has the simple answer to all of our questions, and the rest will come in increments of time, right on time. We are children of the Universe, and we are meant to be here. Being here means we are to have a life that is co-created with the God of our understanding. It is a personal relationship that we get to have. Take it! Enjoy it! And keep showing up... to the next right thing in your life. It is an incredible, unforgettable ride.

Namaste

NOW YOU HAVE IT! DON'T LOSE IT
Fall of 2015 will be the final book to this trilogy of Spiritual Enlightenment.
Look for: NOW YOU KNOW...LET'S GO!

QUICK REFERENCE

Printed in the United States
by Baker & Taylor Publisher Services